From Chickens to Churches

The J. Earl Mead Story

John C. Shanks, Editor

CROSSBOOKS
PUBLISHING

CrossBooks™
A Division of LifeWay
1663 Liberty Drive
Bloomington, IN 47403
www.crossbooks.com
Phone: 1-866-879-0502

First published by CrossBooks 09/15/2011

ISBN: 978-1-6150-7769-4 (sc)
ISBN: 978-1-6150-7770-0 (hc)

Library of Congress Control Number: 2011923724

Printed in the United States of America

This book is printed on acid-free paper.

Dedication

When one thinks of those to whom this book should be dedicated, so many individuals come to mind that the task becomes almost impossible.

Between 1926 and 1962, many hundreds of committed Sunday School and Training Union workers at Cliff Temple Baptist Church, Dallas, answered the call to duty as J. Earl Mead recruited, trained, and inspired them into service for the Lord.

We have chosen to dedicate this book to these many individuals who came to the point that these gifts of service became their "calling," not just an assignment.

With this level of commitment, these workers and J. Earl Mead built one of the largest educational ministries of their day, and in so doing, helped to further the work of the Lord and His Kingdom. God bless their memory.

About Our Cover Art

The elegantly simple drawing of J. Earl Mead which graces the front cover of this book, rendered lovingly in pen and ink by Frances Shanks, was originally produced as the front cover of a Testimonial Luncheon program. On March 28, 1962, the Dallas Baptist Association honored Mr. Mead shortly before his retirement as Minister of Education at Cliff Temple Baptist Church, having served the congregation for over thirty-six years. The classic and thoughtful pose evokes many happy memories for the people who loved and admired Mr. Mead.

The photo which appears on the back cover was captured in the hallways of Lake Forest Village (formerly known as John Knox Village) in Denton, Texas. In 1979, Lois and J. Earl Mead were among the first residents, spending their retirement years there. While in residence, Mr. Mead was named "Chaplain for Life," ministering to and in fellowship with his fellow neighbors and friends. Many happy days of discovery were spent there, exploring and blazing trails around the grounds and the lake on the property and enjoying the wonders of nature as he had done throughout his life. Like his father, A. C. Mead, before him, this was a familiar stance for Mr. Mead --- hands clasped behind him as he walked along, either deep in thought or quietly humming a tune.

Contents

Preface

From Chickens to Churches is the life story of Dr. James Earl Mead, "The General," as he was lovingly called by the staff at Cliff Temple Baptist Church, Dallas. The staff held him in such high regard that a life story was requested of him. This autobiographical story was finished in 1978.

Previous to that date, in 1958, Dr. John Shanks, who served with Dr. Mead at Cliff Temple for eight years, wrote a series of articles about him in the Cliff Temple church paper. Dr. Shanks, along with Lois and Earl Mead, had toured all the locations of Dr. Mead's life and background and wrote the articles as a tribute to Dr. Mead, a Baptist giant of that day.

This book includes the older (1958) articles, Dr. Mead's own autobiography (1978), information concerning his places of service and honors, as well as personal remembrances of him from his grandchildren. These pages are written and edited so that the story of this godly man's life will bless and challenge all who read it.

John C. Shanks, PhD., Editor
Janice Shanks
Margaret Alice Johnson Drake
Martha Lynne Johnson Thrasher
Mead Johnson

About the Editor

John Clinton Shanks is a Dallas native who, early in life at a Baptist encampment, felt a call to vocational Christian service. After graduating from Baylor University, his first full-time call was to Cliff Temple Baptist Church in Dallas. It was his privilege to serve under Dr. Wallace Bassett and to work daily under the mentorship of J. Earl Mead. It was a "match made in heaven" to learn from and to work with this incomparable servant of the Lord. Shanks' second son was named for him ---Drayton Earl Shanks.

While serving in churches full-time or in a bio-vocational position, he received his Master's degree from Southern Methodist University and his PhD from the University of North Texas. He served in churches in Dallas, Wichita Falls, and Longview, Texas, and spent several months in England, preaching and serving as a supply pastor and in other endeavors. He also served in positions with the Annuity Board (now Guidestone) and with Seminary Extension work throughout the state.

Part I

The J. Earl Mead Story

As Written by John C. Shanks in 1958
Published in the *Cliff Temple Baptist*
The Weekly Newspaper of
Cliff Temple Baptist Church
Dallas, Texas

August 29, 1958

About Mead Articles—an Introduction

In the next several issues of your *Cliff Temple Baptist,* you will have the opportunity of reading in brief form some of the outstanding events in the life of our Minister of Education, James Earl Mead. The author, John Shanks, claims no biographical prowess. He simply has a deep feeling that the story of this man's life should be recorded in the files of the records of Cliff Temple Baptist Church; it has already been filed in the lives of many hundreds of thousands of people who have been helped because of their contact with this man of God.

A project like this, kept at a very simple level, still entails some research. Those who are especially responsible for making the collecting of this material possible are: Mrs. Charles R. Moore, Mr. Harry G. Brown, Mr. Rouse Howell, and Mr. Jack N. Roper. Also responsible are many of the relatives and friends of Mr. Mead in Fairplay, Missouri; Cherokee, Oklahoma; Carmen, Oklahoma; Wakita, Oklahoma; Shreveport, Louisiana; Beaumont, Texas; and Dallas, Texas.

August 29, 1958

From Small Beginnings

As the world measures, a man would have to plan diligently to have a much smaller start in life than did James Earl Mead. As is the case with many of the stalwart men of our day, he was born in a humble log cabin. This cabin, being planted in the midst of the stump infested hill country of Polk County, Missouri, near the community of Fairplay, was not much. But it was all that young A. C. Mead and his bride could claim. If the cabin was worth little, the furnishings were worth still less. Yet, these people were possessors of an immense wealth. This wealth, measured in courage and spiritual discernment, was not negotiable at the local bank. But it has been converted into three useful lives which have come from the marital union of A. C. and Vida Amanda Smith Mead. These three lives are J. Earl Mead and his two lovely sisters, Mrs. Zora Mead Haubold and Mrs. Wilma Mead Bramel.

Calloway Mead still blushes a little when his son Earl brags of winning the first and only footrace he ever had with his father. The elder Mead had instructed his wife to raise a white flag as a signal to call him home from the fields if she felt the need of the family doctor. No doubt it was a nervous farmer who topped the hill time and again that day to turn his team and check on the status of events at home. Sure enough, on one of those trips to the brow of the hill, A. C. Mead saw the flag waving in the brisk spring breeze. He dropped his plowing with what seemed to him lightning speed and headed for the doctor's house. But when the two returned, little Earl had already checked in, bag and baggage, and claimed his corner of the one big room. The date in the old Almanac read, April 27, 1892. Thus, with little public note, began a happy childhood chock full of memories which would serve as a foundation for the building of a man, who, in his prime would lead hundreds and thousands closer to Christ.

It was in these early, unknown, and seemingly insignificant days that he learned to love the beautiful things of life. To listen to the song of the birds, to wade the rippling streams, and follow the wandering trails of the mountains of Southern Missouri, seemed to him to be the purpose and end of life itself. No wonder that even today, his every expression of life is a seeming response to the beauty around him. So consuming is that sense of beauty in his life that no force seems powerful enough to replace it with the trivial things of a mere existence. One cannot hope to understand this about the man until he has wandered these Missouri trails, listened to the singing brooks, and risen early to hear the sun say good morning to the world. Also, one could not hope to feel the force of this man's life until he had first himself tried to walk close to God.

If simplicity is indeed a virtue, perhaps one of the greatest contributions to the life of young Earl came through his contact with his clansmen of the hills. Many are the pleasant experiences of the childhood of this man, who discovered life in a community untainted by the rush of urban society as we know it today. It was not unusual to find him, in the company of a cousin, tripping along the fence rows, looking for hazel nuts or running down the pleasant lane to the "middle tree," a spot mid-way between his own home and a house where many of his cousins lived. This tree was the meeting place for the planning of all the social events for the family, and the family was just about the entire community.

Were cousins Minnie and Earl to meet at that tree today, they could have great fun telling again of the time when little Earl notched his dog's tail so he could find him in case he ever wandered away. Then, when the conversation flowed more freely, Mr. Mead would probably admit stealing an apple once, and even cheating in a spelling contest. But one gets the feeling that these experiences will never be forgotten and that great lessons were learned from them.

As one talks with these hill people, he observes quickly some of the finest qualities of life. What is it about them which made such a lasting impression for good on the life of a Christian leader? The simplicity in the lives of these people is only excelled by their profound honesty and faith. A living testimony to this fact can be seen in the words of old Aunt Aggie Mead when she was asked if she were afraid to live alone after her husband died. In the vernacular of the hills, she replied, "I don't live alone! Me and Gawd A'Mighty live here."

Earl is as proud of these hill country relatives as if they were residents of the Presidential Mansion in Washington, as well he might be. They gave him a secure foundation on which to build an honest life of service. Though one of his cousins bears a striking resemblance to Abraham Lincoln, in reality, there was not one of his kin folks who could offer position or wealth in these hills. But from the hills, J. Earl Mead received something for which there is no substitute--character.

His sisters, his cousins, his aunts, and his father, still agree that this boy, whose rearing was begun in the rugged hills of Missouri, was indeed and in reality a man with a soft heart. Being deeply sensitive to the emotions of the human soul made it an easy matter for tears to come to his eyes or a smile to come to his lips. Perhaps this within itself was an indicator of a life that was to come in which hundreds would share their happy moments and their sorrows with this counselor.

September 5, 1958

Early Impressions toward God

Unchanged in a changing world, the little white church house still sits in Polk County, Missouri. It was in this place, "about the middle pew east of the stove," where Earl Mead sat, sometimes to listen and sometimes to sleep, as cousin Minnie Mead attempted to teach him the things of the Lord.

Like the community, Bismont church too was almost a family affair. "Aunt Aggie," says Earl, "married my father's brother. Since she was already related to us by virtue of the fact that she was my maternal grandmother's sister, this made my father's brother his uncle by marriage." Those who have known the hill country in the days of travel by horse and buggy will not wonder that this could be. Even today, with the speed of modern transportation, the creeks and rivers of this area are not choked with the smoke of factories, and little ever happens except morning, noon, and night.

In this pastoral scene pervaded by tranquil beauty, young Earl roamed the banks of these creeks with his cousins or his Uncle Will. Uncle Will, a boy near his own age, was often his partner in mischief. So deep was the affection between these two that it is said when one was visiting the other, he would hide in the barn or the dog house to keep from going home when his parents left; this close feeling has carried through the years.

A foreigner to these Missouri hills would never connect the creek signs he sees along the highway with the pronunciations given by the home folk. To them Barren Creek becomes "Barn Creek;" the Big and Little Sack become "Big and Little Sock!" Together with Bear Creek, these streams still, whispering with memories, flow by the "big road" up a ways from the house. And if one stands in these hills with J. Earl Mead and listens to him spin yarns told to him by his maternal grandfather, he dreams back through the years and suddenly feels 100 years old. He can almost see the hunting trips, the struggles to till the virgin land, the fishing excursions, the happy family get-togethers, and the slaves tied arm to arm marching down the big road toward the South. All of these unique experiences on the threshold of a new age in American History served to make of J. Earl Mead a man who would be an individual in the midst of a throng.

Even the opportunity to learn has always seemed to Earl Mead an opportunity to develop oneself for better service. It was in this little community near Fairplay, where he lived until he was 11 years old, that he received his first education. Few children of our day would understand the procedure at Pickle School, where young Earl was tutored from 1899 to 1903. There were no grades in this school, where a boy could go to school as long as he wanted or quit when he got ready, with the approval of parents. And if a six year old felt capable of challenging the six foot village dullard in ciphering exercises (a contest to determine who was most adept at working math problems), the teacher would welcome the prospect. Earl remembers such an experience when he successfully matched wits with Finus Watkins, a boy who towered above him at the chalk rail.

This closely knit Mead clan has always believed in prayer, and practiced their belief. Once, when the Bismont Church was meeting in the schoolhouse, the pastor, L. F. Simmons, prevailed upon Uncle Tom Mead to give an acre of land so that the congregation might have a building in which to worship. When Uncle Tom was a little reluctant to reduce his estate by the suggested amount, the parson asked him to pray about the matter. After prayer, two acres were given.

The experiences of the farmer in his efforts to live upon the land also had their influence upon young Earl Mead; he learned quickly what it means to live and to grow. He also learned more quickly than he would have chosen that we reap whatever we plant. This truth was burned into his heart, if not into his seat, in a little old cornfield on his grandfather's farm, where he moved with his parents shortly after birth. He and Cousin Ray had been given equal portions of corn in two buckets and had been told they could do what they wished when the corn was planted. Little Earl was surprised to see his cousin, after a short period of time, drop his bucket and "skin" over the fence for home; Earl's corn was only half planted. How could this have happened? All the surprise was dispelled some days later when Calloway Mead escorted both boys back to the "scene of the crime" where all of Ray's corn had come up in one spot. Whether or not Earl had any part in this, (he denies that he did), he learned a lesson.

Calloway Mead vows to this day that Earl was the best boy he ever had. And he vows with such conviction that it takes on meaning even though there were no other boys in the family. "Only whipped me once," says Earl, "between the barn and the smokehouse." But the elder Mead only sits and scratches his head and says, "I can't remember ever having to whip that boy."

September 12, 1958

Go West, Young Man

The words of Horace Greely, advising young America to move west, rang like a clarion call in the ears of A. C. Mead and his father-in-law, J. C. Smith, in the late 1800s. So inviting was the vision of opportunity to these hearty souls that, in 1903, they were willing to exchange the security they had carved out for themselves in the hill country for a try at better things. They hoped also to attempt to recover the health of Grandmother Smith, who was tormented by asthma.

When the little train pulled out of the station at Fairplay on that cold January afternoon, carrying the Mead and Smith clans, practically the entire citizenry of Polk County was present to bid them good bye. After all, these beloved relatives and friends were moving to a place almost 400 miles distance from Fairplay. When such terrible distances were involved in that early day, there was always a degree of finality about the word "good-bye." For an evening, a night, and the entire following day, the little steam engine wound a black ribbon toward the Oklahoma Territory.

At long last, puffing and chugging, the little iron horse reached the Oklahoma strip. They were now in a territory which had been open for settlement for only ten years; it was still occupied principally by prairie dogs, owls, and coyotes. Much of its soil, covered still by blue stem grass, had never seen the ground breaking implements devised by man. Here the two clans would settle together for a spell on a section of land purchased by Grandfather Smith on an earlier scouting foray into the West; the 160 acre plot was hard by the brand spanking new community of Lambert, Oklahoma.

All this new area, with the freshness of the West, changed the pattern but not the personality of young Earl Mead. His range became a little wider, his vision became a little broader, and his soul continued ever to grow toward the beautiful things of God. As the greyhounds pursued their game across the wide open spaces, so young Earl always seemed to pursue life with a zest seldom equaled in human personality. As the winds blew free across that wonderful "heart section" of America, they seemed to breathe into the nostrils of a great young lad the very breath of life that would make him a living soul indeed.

In those early days of life, just before and during teenage, Earl was greatly influenced by his Grandfather Smith. It will surprise no one who has known Earl Mead during his days of professional service to learn that J. C. Smith was a man who loved people and was loved by them in return. Nor will it be amazing to know that he was a man who loved nature. Many were the times when the lad Earl boarded the old wagon with his grandfather to go to the creek bank.

It was always a source of concern to Mrs. Smith that her husband spent so much time in fishing. "Paw," she once said, "you're gonna die on the creek bank someday." "Well," said the old man, "can you think of a better place to die?" "I guess not," she said, "but I was just thinking what a job it would be to haul you into town." Needless to say, Paw Smith's fishing habits suffered very little adjustment as the result of such chiding.

Paw Smith had a personality suited to the selling of his viewpoint, whatever that viewpoint might be at a given time. A licensed preacher from early Missouri days, he turned to politics in Oklahoma. He served many years as state representative to the Oklahoma Legislature from Alfalfa County and served sometime later as a County Officer in Alfalfa County; he had received some little experience earlier in politics when he served for four years as Assistant Treasurer in Polk County, Missouri. Many were the "sour grapes" remarks of politicians who were unable to match him at the polls.

Earl still seems to admire this grandfather as much if not more than any of his illustrious ancestors. But he remembers him not so much for the fact that he practiced law and could get the votes of the people as he does for the fact that he once took a man's case without charge when he felt the man to be in the right. He remembers him not so much for the ability he had to trade a mule for eight acres of land, as he does for the fact that he was the Superintendent of his little Sunday School for many years. He remembers with reminiscing devotion, and, all the while, the laws of heredity and environment show their result in the life of J. C. Smith's grandson.

After a few months with his father-in-law, A. C. Mead branched out and bought his own farm near Yewed, Oklahoma. The folks in the little community of Yewed in the center of the "Sooner" strip had named their town Dewey, but upon learning that this name was already taken, they simply reversed the letters. Calloway, Amanda, and their three children stayed on this farm for only a couple of years before moving to the community of Carmen.

During the migrations of his early life, Earl learned to rise early, work hard, and sleep well with a clear conscience. His first job with remuneration came at the bank in Carmen where he was paid a healthy 75 cents per week for sweeping out the bank and making fires; on this fabulous salary it seemed to him he could paint the town red. No doubt this was possible due to the fact that 75 cents would go further then, not to mention the fact that there was not much town to paint. His second financial adventure came when he decided to hire out in the project of keeping Carmen beautiful through mowing lawns; of the result it can only be said, he did not get rich.

While Earl was beginning to make money in the "work-a-day" world, he continued, of course, to take care of his part of the chores at home. Among those chores often came the milking of the cows. This is a job he never minded except in "fly time and cold weather." The old cat, who hung around their barn, was always glad to see Earl do the milking though. Whether it was a poor aim or simply kind generosity, Tabby often got an extra meal when Earl missed the bucket.

September 19, 1958

Big Days in Little Carmen

As Earl Mead, the incomparable student of human personality, has often reminded his audiences, "You can count on a few fingers those who make the most lasting impressions on your life." It was in Carmen, Oklahoma, that Earl met one of those who would play a big role in his early days and make an imprint that would linger through the years. This man was a seemingly ordinary Baptist preacher with a crippled foot, J. L. Bandy.

When A. C. Mead and his family moved from the farm to the little community of Carmen to set up in the poultry and egg business, one of the first things "the head of the house" did was to take his little family to the local Baptist church. It was almost a conviction with him that unless people had been "tampered with," their religion was Baptist and their politics was Republican. At the time the elder Meads made this church affiliation, J. L. Bandy was the pastor of the faithful little flock. Earl, however, was not yet a Christian.

He had made no profession, but the Spirit of the Lord was pulling at the very strings of his heart. As J. L. Bandy's crippled foot pounded the floor, it seemed to him to be a thumping warning of the wrath of God which is to come. But as the prophet's voice rang from the pulpit, it taught him of promises which, through faith, could be had as an alternative to that otherwise inevitable wrath.

"A wonderful revival broke out," says A. C. Mead. Reverend J. L. Taylor, pastor of the Baptist Church in Fairview, Oklahoma, had been invited to conduct the services in a protracted meeting. Earl was gloriously converted! He almost literally came forth from the baptismal pond with

13

his left hand waving, leading music in his little church. "But though I went to work for God's Kingdom almost immediately," says Earl Mead, "I never would have launched out into the depths had not J. L. Bandy encouraged me."

Little did A. C. Mead's young son dream when he began "throwing" his left arm about, counting time and leading the "saints" at the little Baptist Church at Carmen in congregational singing, that his effort would lead him to a place of immeasurable service in one of the great religious bodies of all time. Nor does he seem to realize it now that he has reached such a place. His sincerity, humility, and devotion keep him too busy to worry about award or position. "But," one catches himself asking, "Isn't this as God intended it?"

In 1911 Earl graduated from the High School at Carmen. Recently, when he went back to that little North Central Oklahoma town for a visit, over half his graduating class met him for a reunion. But this was quite simple since there were only five in the class at the beginning. Earl does not remember who the valedictorian was, doesn't even remember whether they had one, or if they knew what such a "critter" was. But he graduated! With diploma in hand, he went forth to meet the world.

In that early day in the country, American "hillbillyism" had a tight clutch on the land and quartet singing of a certain variety was a rage. In the never ending but always interesting series of circumstances which work out God's will for a man's life, Earl attracted a group of men who wanted him to go to the big city of Fort Worth and study music. "We hear," they said, "there is a professor there by the name of Dr. Uncel. We think he could do wonders for you." So it was off to Fort Worth for young musician Mead. He needed to sit at the feet of one who could teach a person music in three easy weeks and one hard payment.

After about a month of concentration and consternation, Dr. Uncel pronounced young scholar Mead a reasonable subject for graduation. A large and impressive certificate was prepared, and the ledger book was checked to be sure all bills were paid. Things were made ready for the graduation day. Now that the course had been completed and Earl himself was a professor, he donned his cravat, his plug hat, and his turned back collar and set out to impart his knowledge to others. In the summer of 1910, he traveled through many communities of the Texas Panhandle, teaching music schools. He readily admits today that there was very little musical theory left behind when he bade the people farewell and left the community. He also recalls that there was little remuneration to such effort. But expenses were met, and all had a very wonderful time. During this period, the budding young education director actually wrote a few songs, but he doesn't recall the names of them today; nor can they readily be found in the hymnals!

Though all such experiences were, in the long run, really a side track for Earl Mead, they were not a waste of time. Through them, he continued to learn people--how to love them, how to work with them, and how to lead them. He learned that the best way to get a job done was to organize immediately and address oneself to the tasks at hand.

During all this time, it will be remembered, religion was still an avocation with Earl Mead. Though he went with J. L. Bandy to lead music in revivals in several towns, including Saint Louis, he still worked in the church just because he loved it and felt obliged to be of service. Quite a young man now, Earl was in business with his father.

Earl's first duty in the poultry and egg business with his dad, where he would spend several years of his early life, was building egg cases. Even this he did well. Always has he shown that quality of application of himself to any task before him. It is said that he could build 200 cases in one day. At 1 ½ cents per case, this meant that he made $3.00 per day; to a teen-aged lad, this was almost a windfall.

In 1911, now 19 years of age, Earl was called upon to make another adjustment in life. His father purchased a poultry and egg business in Wakita, Oklahoma, and Earl and the other members of the family were called upon to sever close friendships developed in the course of some seven years, and move to a new town. Perhaps we can begin to see through so many varied experiences why Earl has always thought things are never incidental or accidental and that all the chapters of life make a beautiful story when we let God do the writing.

September 26, 1958

Never Say "Growed"

Earl Mead has always had a holy dissatisfaction with himself. Perhaps this is the reason he has always sought to develop his talents; perhaps this is the reason he enrolled in the business college in Wichita, Kansas, in 1912; perhaps this is the reason for a lot of things he has done in life. Young Earl was "dead set" on the idea of enrolling in school in the fall of 1912 to stretch his gray matter a bit. Calloway thought his boy was a bit all right as he was, and besides that, he would be just about as handy as buttons on a shirt in helping with the poultry and peddling eggs. But, being a man of gentle kindness and consideration, the elder Mead could not bring himself to question or criticize his boy's decision. However, after the schooling had been completed, and only then, Calloway mustered enough courage to ask shyly if his son felt the adventure had been worth the value extended. Earl, of course, replied that he thought without question it had been of an inestimable value.

Three or four decades ago in mid-America, regular college training as we know it now, was a rarity. Folks with Master's Degrees, and sometimes those with Bachelor's, were viewed as something as unusual as the animals at a city zoo. The emphasis was more on practical training which could be specifically applied to one's trade. Thus, Earl felt the Business College in Wichita was just the place for a man developing a poultry trade. Let it be known though that this school did offer, in addition to straight business courses, some training in English and other such cultural and academic areas. "In fact," says Earl, "it was in Wichita that I learned most of the English which was to set me in good stead for my correspondence in the poultry business and for my latter public speaking in religious education." He can still hear the teacher repeating over and over, "Never say growed, throwed, blowed, or busted."

In his two years at the business college, Earl excelled again. This time, the group was a more sizable one. Of 300 people, Earl was first in rapid calculation. With trigger-like crispness, his mind came up with the answers to problems presented it. His shorthand was so very rapid that a teacher was assigned alone to him for a while in an attempt to prepare him for court reporting. But, about this time, Earl fell in love! And there seemed to be a perfect negative correlation between his love affair and his speed in shorthand. As Cupid soared, the possibility of court reporting drooped. Interestingly enough, the name of the girl has long since been forgotten. But, one has to admit again, when Earl Mead does a thing, there is no reservation.

There is, it is to be recognized, a question which will worm its way into the thoughts of all who have received hand penned notes from Earl Mead. For these gems, scrawled with a left hand full of love, are at times real puzzles to decipher. "Why," it will be asked, "didn't they do something about his handwriting while they were trying to 'spruce' him up a bit?" Well, the answer is, THEY DID! But it did not take! The fact is Earl's writing is so poor that he took typing so that he could be more formal when the occasion demanded. But, it is thought by at least some, his writing was so especially unusual that it probably had a negative effect even on his typing! To say the least, "Old Lefty" could not seem to be helped with his penmanship!

So, Earl Mead graduated, for the third time. He felt far more qualified now to go back to Wakita and help his dad in their fowl (be careful of the spelling, he says) business. His higher qualifications were put to use very shortly as his father was to engage in the poultry and egg business in Anthony, Kansas, and then in Caldwell, Kansas. When this happened, the business at Wakita was left under the guiding hand of young business graduate Earl Mead. Small profits were very important with prices as they were. A few cents one way or another would determine whether a man made money or went broke. With ducks selling for 10 to 15 cents per piece, not to mention the fabulous price of 12 to 13 cents per dozen on eggs, Earl had to address himself to his business with a zeal that would not die. After all, his father was depending on him. It was his father's capital matched with Earl's skill that made that long-to-be-remembered partnership. So hard did he work that this business was fairly engrained into his soul. He is still almost willing today to match a man in a race to see who can do the speediest and best job of candling eggs.

Young Earl was such a success that one of his nephews observed that Wakita was a fine place for the wholesaling of poultry and eggs, and so he would just go into business against his southpaw uncle. With his quick ingenuity, Earl was almost immediately selling eggs and poultry for less than his nephew was able to buy. Needless to say, the nephew soon gave up his doubtful adventure as a bad one. He sold out, to add insult to injury, to his Uncle Earl.

Even with all this business adventure in progress, Earl still had time for his church work. Soon after he had arrived at Wakita from Carmen, for that matter, he had begun to lead the little church's choir. And such a fine job was done the choir was often asked to present the special music for associational meetings and other programs.

Earl had a larger and ever larger place in his heart for the Lord and the church, but, he admits, the Lord still had not come close to his pocket book or his life like he felt He should. "I was quick to 'Amen' Dan Curb's sermon on tithing when he came to preach in a week's revival at our little church. But when he got around to making the personal application to my own life, I became strangely silent." Dan Curb, a pastor in the association, traveled about some in that earlier day preaching Dr. Gambrell's sermon, "Who Owns the Wool." Earl and all others readily agreed that it was God. But the difficulty came when the sermon presented shearing time as a time to tithe. The final crushing blow came when the preacher reminded his audience that at shearing time, the sheep could be distinguished from the goats because of their lack of resistance.

October 3, 1958

The Lady Wore Green

More Groom, less gloom
Bright moon, no spoon.

She crooned a tune,
That healed my wound.

I sighed and crooned
Of brides and June.

She gasped, "So soon?"
"Ere flowers bloom."

We'll seal our doom
As bride and groom.
---J. Earl Mead

It was a windy fall day in 1914 that James Earl Mead first laid eyes on Alice Groom from Winfield, Kansas. As fate would have it, she had come to Wakita to visit a sister. This astute young business man was evidently looking at girls instead of eggs that morning when she passed down the street. Blushingly he admits, "I noticed the green pantaloons, way down around her ankles," he hastens to add. But whatever it was that won his heart, her striking beauty, her gentle kindness, or her winning personality of sincere sweetness, Earl had been "taken."

To be fair to the male sex, evidence seems to indicate that Alice was just as smitten with Earl as he was with her. In fact, just by coincidence of course, she came to live with her sister in Wakita in the winter of 1914; somehow a job had opened up for her in the little town.

The trips which Earl made between Wakita and Winfield before Alice moved to Wakita, however, indicated that a real love affair was blossoming into full reality. As usual, Earl wasted no time when his mind was settled. He very soon began to prod Alice to press his case with her father. Of course, the two were well into their twenties at the time; but, in that day, no one would think of engagement or marriage without first consulting parents. Being a little shy, Alice hesitated to approach her big six-foot-plus father.

One evening as the two were "courtin" in the parlor of the Groom home, Earl began to ask Alice what she thought her father would say about their desires toward marriage. She said that she really didn't know but that her father was sitting in the next room. "I'll tell you what," said Earl, "I just believe I'll ask him." With this he called in loud tones, "Oh, Mr. Groom." In a flash, Alice went completely limp in a dead faint. Earl continued, "What time does that next train leave for Wakita?" Needless to say, Alice could have murdered him on the spot. He had almost literally scared her out of a year's growth. But Earl did approach her father, by way of U. S. mail, when he returned to Wakita. And, soon after this, plans were begun for the marriage which would take place in June of 1915, only 8 months or so after their original and unusual meeting.

Earl Mead, in the meantime, went about his business of running the poultry house in the little community of Wakita. But, all the while, the song on his lips was gayer, the gleam in his eye was brighter, and the cockles of his heart were warmer. As he has often said, "Who likes cold cockles anyway?" The people of the community must have noticed this change in Earl, and some probably even suspected what was about to take place. But no official word had been spoken. All secrecy was betrayed though one day when the local drayman received a shipment of furniture to outfit an entire house; the shipment was directed to Miss Alice Groom. Certainly she could not be using all this furniture if she planned to continue living with her sister. Now there are several forms of communication in small towns. Among these is the party line telephone, with so many long and/or short signals to let everyone in the community know who it is preparing to converse; there is also the local weekly or "weakly" newspaper. But, of the two leading media, telephone and "tell-a-lady," one will readily have to admit that the latter is much more effective. When a few of the ladies in the community heard the news, all Wakita soon knew that a wedding would take place shortly.

Now Earl has always, along with his complete dependence upon the Lord, also had a personal feeling of independence in as far as his fellows are concerned. He wanted to rent his house, furnish it, and marry right there; this he did. His close friends and family know that only one thing always did "cramp his style" just a little. Alice, being a few months older than he, took it that she had lived longer and could give him a little free advice occasionally on matters of the world and philosophy. "And, by gum-it," he says, "I knew it just wasn't so." But Earl always loved, for she deserved his love, his "gentle Alice." Before they were married, he penned the following words to her:

MEDITATION

As I sit alone and ponder,
O'er vicissitudes of life,
My mind is wont to wander,
To the future and My Wife.

The darkness gathers 'round me,
Brings meditations sweet'
The fire-light seems to hound me,
With visions hard to beat.

The gentle zephyrs whisper,
In melancholy tone,
And causes me to miss her,
While sitting here alone.

I close my eyes in silence,
While visions most sublime,
Steal o'er me in compliance,
To memories divine.

That hair, those eyes, her beauty,
Her every look and act,
Are pictured there to suit me,
And nothing does she lack.

The dearest of God's creatures ---
A Goddess does she seem,
As all her heav'nly features,
Are pictured in my dream.

I cross the Bridge of Patience,
That spans the Stream of Time;
My mental vision hastens,
To picture her as mine.

I revel in contentment,
In happiness serene,
For this is the commencement,
Of REAL life with My Queen.

When reality had budded,
From this dream-world of mine,
Life's pathway will be studded,
With happiness sublime.

My reverie is broken,
My mind has ceased to roam,
Reality has spoken,
Of you, Sweetheart and Home.
---J. Earl M.

October 10, 1958

From the Valleys of Decision

From the valleys of trial and decision always come the men who climb the highest and stand the straightest atop the "mountain peaks" of service to humanity. And there is just a vague possibility that Earl Mead is considered "father-confessor" to hundreds of education men and even preachers today because of the difficult decisions of his own life, coupled with the hilarious moments, of course. It seems that life to him has always been on the topmost point of the mountain's brow or in the lowest depths of its valley below. Perhaps this variety is the thing which has so spiced his life that he can usually see tragedy with a smile and view success with a somber note of thanksgiving.

Earl and Alice had been married for only a few brief months when the glad news came that their home would be blessed with one of God's choicest gifts, a baby. And many were the happy hours spent in preparation for the arrival of this expected addition. As young Earl worked still a little harder to provide food and clothing for the new one, Alice spent her time sewing and dreaming. "Will it be a boy or will it be a girl? Will it look like Earl, or will it look like me? Oh, well, what's the difference? It's going to be ours and we will be so thankful!"

And then, on May 14, 1916, the lovely little bright-eyed baby came and she was named Lois Maxine. There was such joy and happiness for the moment in the Mead's house that nothing else in all the world seemed to matter. But things did not go well with Alice. Very soon after the baby was born, Alice began to have fever. And, as the hours came and went her condition seemed to worsen. Then, one night, Earl heard the two local doctors in consultation about Alice's condition; they knew that things had gotten out of hand. They were ready to admit that unless she was better by morning, they wanted more skilled hands to take charge. "If my beautiful young bride will possibly need more skilled hands in the morning, she needs them now," Earl decided. He informed the doctors immediately on his decision and they readily agreed. The skilled hands were secured, and the family was informed that an operation must be performed at once! Blood poisoning had begun!

Wakita was a long way from the big city, and Alice was a very sick young lady; she could not be moved, for there was not time and she did not possess the physical strength. The surgeon's instruments were made ready. A supply of boiling water was prepared. The dining room was quickly transformed into a hospital with the big table serving as an operating table. As the delicate hand of the physician carefully displayed its skill, Earl paced the floor like a young caged lion. After two grueling hours, which seemed like an eternity to the young father, the surgeon placed aside the tools of his profession and left the recovery in the hands of the Lord.

For some days Alice mended slowly and then with more rapidity. It seemed now to Earl that the world's symphony of experiences once again played a beautiful melody. There was a song in his heart, and the stars seemed to shine just a little more brightly at night. But then, in the midst of the music, the drums of fate rolled with a thundering crescendo as the young baby was also brought low from the poison which had been transmitted to her from her mother's body. First it seemed that Alice would die! Now it seemed that the baby might not live! Could there be any more crushing burdens brought to the shoulders of this young man? To him it did not seem possible! Lois Maxine improved and became healthy again! But the mind of God knew that other burdens were still to follow.

But these burdens only served to prove the fiber of this young lad. It was actually in the midst of all these experiences that Dan Curb came to preach his tithing sermon at Wakita, and Earl decided to quit bargaining with God. After all the doctor bills were paid and the ledger sheets were balanced, Earl found that he was in debt $2,000.00. To him, and for that day, this was staggering. He figured that it would take him three years to come clear. But, in it all, he decided not to use God's money to pay his debts. "This," he says, "was one of the most profitable experiences of a lifetime for me." Though he is quick to remind that we never tithe for the purpose of receiving blessings from God, he also says that God has done more through him with the ninety percent than he could have done alone with 100 per cent. At the end of one year, his business was in the black again.

During all this time, Earl's father Callaway was busily engaged in the operation of the poultry house at Anthony, Kansas. Actually still in the prime of his career, his energy was untiring. But Callaway's wife, in spite of her comparative youth, was not well. It appeared more and more obvious as the time passed, that she would soon receive her summons to meet the Lord. Her devoted husband stayed close at hand, as did her three loving children.

It was during the time that she was on her death bed that Earl Mead's mother provided him with an experience he can never escape from; nor does he care to do so. Seeming to know that the end was very near, she called her husband, her children, and her father to her bedside. When they had taken their places round about her, she asked that each one voice a brief prayer. After this had transpired, she asked Earl to go to the piano and play and sing her favorite hymn, "Nothing between My Soul and the Savior." Though this was one of the hardest jobs he had ever done, he accomplished the great ordeal bravely. Very soon afterward, her soul went to be with the Lord whom she loved.

If there ever had been "dross" in his soul, the "fires of life" had now burned it away. The lad had become a full grown man. The uncertain Christian was able to work more closely and more definitely with the Master. But Earl Mead was still just a short time away from what turned out to be the most significant crossroad of decision in his entire life.

October 17, 1958

A Way Unknown

In the second decade of the twentieth century, a young Baptist encampment was born in Oklahoma; it was named Falls Creek. From its ordinary beginnings when it was known only locally in that fair state, it has come now to be a traditional place known to all throughout the Southern Baptist Convention. Whereas it drew a group considered to be quite a fair number in that early day, it has come now to its present drawing ability of several thousand souls each year. Earl Mead led the music in this encampment in its second and third years of existence. It was during the third year that he faced the crossroads of his life.

No doubt, the Lord Himself felt that Earl Mead's experiences had well prepared him for the job for which He had for him to do. As the committee preparing the program for Falls Creek seemed to hit a snag that year in the matter of someone to lead the singing, the missionary of the Salt Fork Valley Association spoke. Little did this missionary, H. E. Hogan by name, realize that he was having a part in starting one of the most colorful careers of Southern Baptist history when he said, "Why not let Earl Mead of Wakita do it again?"

In Mr. Mead's own words, "I knew little about music and nothing about education." But, since this effort at Falls Creek still seemed to Earl just the effort of a layman to serve the Lord, he was willing to give it another "whirl." Of course, as one looks back now, he can see the pattern falling into place piece by piece. And, as is often true, God, in this case, led a young man to the beauties of nature at Falls Creek to lay a burden upon his heart.

"There are no incidentals or accidentals in the life of a man who puts himself in God's hands." This is a statement often made by Earl Mead through his years of service in Christian education. He probably learned this first at Falls Creek, when he met a man who had just been called to be pastor of the First Baptist Church of Beaumont, Texas. The man, A. E. Booth, shocked Earl Mead to the very foundation of his soul by telling him he wanted him to come to Beaumont as Director of Music and Education. To the young poultry-man, it was a way unknown! But as he thought about it and prayed about it, he knew that the unknown way would be better than a known way, if it were God's will.

As the days passed, the impression grew stronger in Earl's mind till he came to the point where he decided to "burn all the bridges" behind him and surrender his will to the Lord. He would accept! By this time, Earl was talking pretty seriously to his father about their business arrangements which were about to be affected. "Son," said Callaway, "you can keep your interest in the business just in case things don't work out." "No, Dad," said young Earl, "I'm not going into this to fail the Lord. There will be no turning back."

As things moved rapidly now, there were many family adjustments to be made also. Alice was a Methodist, and Earl had never seen fit to try to force her into a decision which did not originate in her own thinking. Though she had attended the Baptist Church at Wakita with Earl since their marriage, she had never felt like making the official change. But as she viewed the prospect of being the wife of a church worker, Alice knew that she must be a part of every area of his life; she made the decision to join the church with Earl, and it was her own decision. This was a thing which made the young husband quite happy. Everything seemed to be working out now as it should. And so, in the fall of 1919, J. Earl Mead became a pioneer in a young profession seldom heard of until fairly recent days. And even as recently as 1919, when he entered the field, Mr. Mead's name appeared on the letter head as Assistant to the Pastor; the term Education Director, if it had been coined, was seldom used.

Among Mr. Mead's first close associates at Beaumont were two young boys who are known now as the pastors of the First Baptist Church of Springfield, Missouri, and the Parker Memorial Baptist Church of Anniston, Alabama. Now mature Christian leaders, they are Dr. Fred Eastham and Rev. B. Locke Davis. As has been the case through all his years of service, Earl was quick to attract young people and bring out their best.

Actually, though, it took a little doing for Earl to attract these two boys, especially Dr. Eastham. The prominent Southern Baptist pastor recalls with amusement the first time he ever laid eyes on Earl Mead.

"His pants were too short and too tight," says Eastham. "And as I watched him wave that left hand about in what appeared to me a feeble attempt to lead the music, I turned to B. Locke Davis to tell him that I didn't think Mr. Mead would ever make it." Dr. Eastham now gets the heartiest chuckle of all when this story is repeated.

To balance the ledger, Mr. Mead has some recalling of his own to do when the name Fred Eastham is mentioned. "That boy took me on my first and last duck hunt," says Earl. "After getting me lost in one of the marshes around Beaumont, he nearly froze me to death by having me squat in the cold water every time a duck flew over. And, to make it worse, they all flew over so high that we had no success at all that day." Except for that one time, Earl Mead always has preferred to study birds rather than to hunt them.

One can travel back to many of the churches of the Southeast Texas Baptist Association today thirty-nine years after J. Earl Mead arrived on the scene, and find people whom he put to work, still working. "This," says Earl Mead, "is the real joy of a life spent attempting to serve the Lord. If such is a waste of life, then all my life has been wasted!"

Though the days at Beaumont were deeply happy ones, this experience too had its keenly sad moments. While in his first experience at Beaumont, Mr. Mead was almost tempted to turn back and forget forever his new-found field of service.

October 24, 1958

A Church--Conflict and Resolution

On the first of September in 1919, J. Earl Mead and his little clan moved to Beaumont to assume the position of Assistant to the Pastor with the fabulous salary of $150.00 per month. "And we lived on it," he says. "The fact of the business is, the amount seemed rather large at the time," he continues. "But I always have wondered just a little about the circumstances of my hiring. The pastor had told his folks he had found a man at Falls Creek who could handle this job. So, without the church ever seeing me, the hiring was done. I guess we both took quite a chance, now that I look back on the matter."

But it didn't take long for the entire city of Beaumont to fall in love with the 27 year old young man and his beautiful young wife and three-year-old daughter. For the next four years, the days were filled with activity. There were the sessions at the Southeast Texas Baptist Association Encampment, where the young man met his two future pastors, M. E. Dodd and Wallace Bassett; there were the hilarious times when big groups of Beaumont-ers boarded the train, armed with banners and yells, and headed for the state encampment at Palacios; and, of course, there were the wonderful times of teaching and fellowship in the church itself. But then came the time of storm. For the next two years, only the faith of a man like J. Earl Mead could have been adequate refuge for his own soul and for the life of the church itself. The pastor's home was broken up, and the waves of unrest rolled in an overwhelming tide.

It was in this seemingly impossible atmosphere that the young giant Mead stood and silenced forever the damaging tongues of careless

Christians who would have continued to discuss matters which could only bring hurt to the Lord's cause. As Earl Mead stood on a Wednesday night, in an electrified crowd, he disarmed them and made of them a harmonious group. Taking as his text the story of Zaccheus' inability to see Jesus because of the press of the crowd, he spoke that night with power from above. And, before the evening had passed, there was a solemn vow between that band of Christians and their Master that never again would pass their lips words of gossip on a matter which should be forgotten forever. "In fact," says Mr. Mead, "many times in the following months, leaders in the convention remarked that nobody in the church would discuss the matter." The church was on the road back.

But it was a long road back. For fourteen months, the church did not have a pastor on the field. During this time, Earl Mead was sent through the fires of trial. This whole situation resulted in keen disappointment for him, and he had to remind himself many times that he really was not walking alone. "During all this time," he says, "I learned anew that my faith must be always in the Lord rather than in any individual, knowing this would be, for any circumstance, the only ballast necessary for the rough spots of life's sea." It is significant that never since this experience has Earl Mead's boat seemed to rock as it did momentarily in that earlier experience.

During most of these difficult days, the church actually had a pastor, but they didn't; this made things even more difficult for the young education director. The uncertainty only added weight to the other burdens of the moment. The church, shortly after their pastor's resignation, had called B. W. Vining, Assistant Executive Secretary of the Baptist General Convention of Texas, to be their pastor. However, shortly after the call was extended, Dr. Vining became ill. And, while he lingered on his death bed, Beaumont continued to consider him as their pastor. The state convention paid half his salary and the First Baptist Church of Beaumont paid the other half until his death several months later. He never preached a sermon as pastor of the church. It seemed to the congregation that one tragedy only invited another.

During all this time, according to many of the people in the congregation, the only thing which saved the church for its present greatness was the big building objective which they had before them, and the leadership of a man named Mead. Before their unfortunate experiences, they had already begun to accumulate funds for the building of a new auditorium. And now, in the absence of a pastor, it would fall to J. Earl Mead to lead the people in the major part of the construction of this building. The building was practically completed when a new pastor arrived at the church in the winter of 1925. "This welded us together," says Earl, "and made us forget things of lesser importance."

In February of 1925, J. H. Pace of Waxahachie became pastor of the First Baptist Church of Beaumont. A nightmare began to end and the dawn of a new day came for the church. J. Earl Mead, now 33, possessed a great deal more wisdom and faith than had been his when he arrived on the scene in the fall of 1919. From Dr. Pace's arrival in February, Mr. Mead stayed with the church until the following September.

In June of 1925, Earl Mead was President of Southeast Texas Baptist Encampment. At that same session, Dr. M. E. Dodd of Shreveport was the camp pastor. Dr. Dodd was attracted to Earl Mead for the same reason Dr. Bassett was attracted to him. Both later admitted they were deeply impressed by his industry and his love and attraction for people. While the camp was in session, Dr. Dodd approached Mr. Mead about coming to Shreveport. And later in the summer, while he was enroute to teach at Siloam Springs, Arkansas, Mr. Mead stopped by to see the church at Shreveport. After praying the matter through in his native Ozarks, he accepted the position.

When the people in Beaumont heard of his decision, they bought him a set of suitcases. "Don't think they meant anything personal," he says. "Anyway, we had a wonderful experience which will always be a part of my life." He has returned many times in the 33 intervening years to see still existing signs of progress made during his six difficult years of leadership.

October 31, 1958

A Man Named Dodd

As the ever-rolling waters of the stream etch out slowly but surely the majestic beauty of the mountain's peak, so the gathering of experiences early in life began to forge the pattern for the man Mead. His association with M. E. Dodd, pastor of the First Baptist Church of Shreveport, must be considered of prime importance when one attempts to evaluate the life of one who is considered by hundreds to be the most successful education director of our generation.

It has been said that no one would be able to work with M. E. Dodd. His driving, forceful, and untiring personality had caused many less successful and less energetic people to play on his initials with the nickname "ME" Dodd. History does reveal that J. Earl Mead's predecessors at First Baptist Church of Shreveport had kept the transfer companies busy moving them in and out of that fair city. Earl Mead was not impressed by this at all! It only served to challenge him to show what could be done.

On September 1, 1925, Mr. Mead began a year of service which has never been forgotten either by the Shreveport church or by Mead himself. In as far as the church was concerned records were set in attendance, which still stand. In as far as the man J. Earl Mead was concerned it was a year in which he learned much about organization, program building, and use of time. "And Dodd was a prince," says Earl. "When he discovered that I didn't mind rolling my sleeves up and going to work, he forgave me of all my other shortcomings. He was a man who believed in much hard work."

One of the instances which has remained in Earl Mead's mind through the years happened one morning in 1926 as Dr. Dodd was presiding over a staff meeting. The business manager in the office of the Shreveport Church was John Ramond. In the course of the agenda for that day, Dr. Dodd turned to Mr. Ramond to request something of him. Quickly Ramond replied, "But Dr. Dodd, I can't ..." The staffer was never allowed to finish his sentence! "Can't," said Dr. Dodd, "is not in the Christian's vocabulary." Ramond proceeded to fulfill the request.

Since Dr. Dodd was such a strong personality and since he was one of America's leading evangelical pulpiteers in those days, the church at Shreveport was quite heavy on preaching compared to its educational emphasis. In fact, this one truth probably had more to do with J. Earl Mead's coming to Cliff Temple than any other one thing. His education program at Shreveport was housed principally in a Lodge Hall, the Y.M.C.A., and the offices of one of the local newspapers. With that being true, it was quite attractive to him when Rev. Wallace Bassett, the 40 year old pastor of the young Cliff Temple Baptist Church in Dallas, told him of his dreams to build a church through the building of an education program.

In December, 1925, G. S. Hopkins resigned the position of Education Director at Cliff Temple to become Sunday School Secretary for the State of Texas. There was no doubt in Wallace Bassett's mind as to the one he wanted to succeed his close friend, Hopkins; he wanted J. Earl Mead of Shreveport. He quickly got his committee together and the approach was made before the first of the year. The committee consisted of G. A. McGregor, now of Lampasas; G. M. West, deceased; Mrs. W. A. Pile of Nashville, Tennessee; Charles R. Moore, deceased; and Mrs. W. H. Bussell, now of San Antonio. As a team, these people set out to get their man.

But J. Earl Mead turned them down! Mr. Mead realized that he had not been at Shreveport but just a very short while. He did not want to do anything that would hurt the work of the church there. But his feeling did not stop the relentless persistence of the committee. Dr. Bassett, as spokesman for the committee, approached Mr. Mead again in February of 1926 at the Organized Class Convention in Birmingham, Alabama. "As long as we feel like we do," the Dallas pastor said, "we are not going to call anyone else." "Well," said Mead, "as long as I feel like I do, I am not coming." Still not being dissuaded, Cliff Temple contacted Earl Mead again in midsummer; again, he turned them down.

But, as the months and days rolled by, they left their weight on the heart of the man. "If they are right," he reasoned, "and I am wrong, what a tragedy it would be." It was in this atmosphere that Dr. Bassett wrote a letter telling Mr. Mead to call by Sunday if he was interested; he did not call. But Sunday night was even a greater battle! Bright and early on Monday morning, and the mornings always have been bright and early with J. Earl Mead, he called Dr. Bassett! When the call was completed, Earl was relieved to discover that the committee, deciding that some action must be taken, had offered the job to George Mason. This, the two men agreed, would be the indication of God's leadership. If Mr. Mason accepted, Mr. Mead would know that he had been right all along. If Mason rejected the offer, then J. Earl Mead would become Education Director of Cliff Temple.

Before the week was out, Mr. Mead accepted the job. And Dr. Bassett, always a man to pursue his objectives with untiring energy and skill, went to Shreveport to be certain that nothing would happen to defeat Cliff Temple's purpose. After all, they had waited for almost a year for this man. But what a wonderful year's wait it was when Cliff Temple looks back now on the 30 plus years of devoted and fruitful service.

When Dr. Dodd, on vacation in Springfield, Ohio, heard the news, he reacted quickly with a telegram. It read, "Surprised, Disappointed, Hurt. You promised me and told the people that Cliff Temple was a closed incident. Your going practically means my end at Shreveport. Am wiring Dr. Bassett. I do not appreciate his persistence. Do nothing further until I return. M. E. Dodd." But, after some time, Dr. Dodd forgave both Mr. Mead and Dr. Bassett for their decision.

November 7, 1958

Beginning Days in a Brilliant Career

The noise of children at play was one of the first attractions to greet J. Earl Mead when he arrived at Cliff Temple in 1926. The area around the church, which has long since become principally business property, was "loaded with young-uns!" And this noise was certainly sweet music in the ears of a man who knew that here he had just what it would take to build a mighty Sunday School. At that time, the community of Boundary (Jefferson and Marlborough) was clear out in the country, and Jimtown (Hampton and Clarendon) was a little community all its own. The church, still a mere "child" of 25 with most of its history in the future, was young and vigorous. The restricting forces of tradition and conservatism were seldom felt! The sky was the limit in what could be accomplished by this band of Christians who were interested in "making tracks." With such an atmosphere, even a lesser man could have achieved. But, with such a prevailing spirit, a man like J. Earl Mead was destined to make history in the education work of the entire Baptist denomination.

When Earl Mead arrived on the scene, work had just been completed on Junior Building, a gym (where Primary Departments are now located on floors one and two of Central Hall), and Christian Hall (formerly Tenth Street Hall). The old auditorium (now our chapel) and Hewitt Hall had been completed sometime before. Shortly after Mr. Mead arrived on the scene, the land where the Temple of Worship now stands was purchased. Many were the happy days and hours spent by all in planning what would be constructed for the Lord on this block. Old timers at Cliff Temple will recall that the plan was originally set for the Temple to face Zang Blvd.

But when the depression of the thirties began to show its force, some of the leadership felt that we might have to sell off some lots on Zang to pay ourselves out of debt; so, the Temple was faced on Tenth Street.

The most severe economic recession this country has felt to date did not daunt the spirit of a man like Mead, nor did it have any noticeable influence on the spirit of his great pastor and comrade of the years, Wallace Bassett. These men, in those days, met each Saturday with the leadership of the church to think of new ways to raise more money and to determine which bills could be delayed for the longest period of time. Twice during these bleak months, the two leaders suggested that their salaries be cut. Both times the deacons accepted the suggestion and reduced the pay. "After that," says Earl Mead, "I never made such a suggestion again."

Of all the educational organizations at the church, the Training Union, for some reason, responded most quickly to Mead's call when he arrived at Cliff Temple. From that response has come leadership now scattered over the entire Southern Baptist Convention. Just before the phenomenal growth of Training Union at Cliff Temple, a church in Sherman, Texas, had been leading the convention in Training Union. "Maybe," recollects Earl Mead, "it can be accounted for like this. After all, there were only about three Baptist churches in our rapidly growing community at that time. The people were here! And we organized to go out and get them. In fact, we were one of the first churches to have multiple departments in Training Union." But regardless of the reason, Cliff Temple led the South in Training Union work for many years. From this period there came, among others, the following Baptist leaders: Bob Wideman, A. D. Walters, Bill Webb, Harvey Nelson, Cornell Goerner, Will T. Dansby, Josephine Pile, Winnie D. Marshall Miller, Chester Hart, and Porter Routh. Also during this period, one of the members of the staff was a young man by the name of R. A. Springer. Little did his colleagues dream that this "boy" who had been hired from a piano company would advance to the position of Treasurer of the Baptist General Convention of Texas. Indeed these were glorious days for the growing young community and church.

As was true in his former positions and also at Cliff Temple, Earl Mead was quick to win the youth to his side. Also, as at Beaumont and Shreveport, this could probably be attributed to some degree to his athletic ability. He has always been most adept at tennis, volleyball, and handball. In fact, when he first came to Dallas, he and J. B. Christian, Sr. became members of a fireman's volleyball team which lost only to the national champions in a Y.M.C.A. playoff. Because this team had to beat a Cliff

Temple team to get to the playoffs, Mr. Mead was nicknamed "Benedict Arnold" and Mr. Christian was nicknamed "Bergdall" (a traitor in World War I). The young athletes at Cliff Temple tried to figure every way in the world to beat this fearsome combination, but to no avail. Of course, it was all in fun, and the youth loved their leaders for their ability to enjoy life.

Under the leadership of Earl Mead, new ideas were injected into the education program. He had already inherited a fine training program which had been set up by his predecessor, G. S. Hopkins. He took this program and extended it a step further to originate what we now call "Back Yard Study Courses;" they were originally called "think-nics." This idea, of course, soon caught on with the state leadership and was eventually extended over the entire convention. In addition, one of J. Earl Mead's "babies" is the "Fall Tee Off." Originally termed an "education rally," this was a thing which attracted much attention in that earlier day. Men would come from far places to see Mr. Mead direct this program. Now, as is well known, most every church has some such special program each fall.

Without question then or now, Mr. Mead's early days at Cliff Temple indicated that men were about to see a brilliant career begin to unfold. They were about to see a soul of extraordinary ability and dedication address himself to a mighty task. And today, to reflect upon it all is sheer inspiration for those who love him, and for those who love to see the Lord's work prosper.

November 14, 1958

Dean of Education Directors

Because of his position in the Baptist Denomination, Mr. Mead is sometimes called the "Dean of Education Directors" in the Southern Baptist Convention. He is sometimes referred to, lovingly, as the "Bishop of Education Directors." Not only do the men in this profession come to him by the hundreds for advice and leadership, the pastors over the South keep his desk loaded with letters asking for advice in the securing of a Minister of Education. This is a position of responsibility which he has never misused. He always considers the confidence placed in him to be a sacred trust. He enters vicariously into all the problems, joys, hurts, and victories which are shared with him.

Earl Mead's place of leadership in the denomination has not come overnight. Nor has the confidence of others been placed in him without careful judgment. Because he has loved, others love him; because he has proved himself a worthy leader, other leaders want to share the secrets of his success. They seek his advice often in the making of their decisions. Thus, through such channels of service, Earl Mead finds himself constantly in the stream of Baptist affairs in his association, state, and throughout the Southern Baptist Convention.

It would be difficult to number the positions J. Earl Mead has held in the Dallas Baptist Association. It is of significance to mention, however, that he was the first Sunday School Superintendent Dallas County Baptists ever elected. In this position of service, he visited each church personally during the tenure of his administration. He was elected President of the Texas Baptist Training Union Convention in 1931 and presided over the conventions which were held in 1932, 1933, and 1934. Almost a decade later he was elected to be President of the Texas Baptist Sunday School Convention; he served in this office during the year of 1941. Between his terms of office at the head of our Sunday School and Training Union work in the state, he served in 1936 as President of the Southwestern Baptist Religious Education Directors Association. During all this time, probably his most significant work was done for the denomination through his service on the first two correlation committees which were ever appointed by the Southern Baptist Convention. These committees were to study our education work. Though they did not realize their dreams immediately, they began a foundation for some of the advancements we are beginning to see in our own hour.

But all of J. Earl Mead's work was not done in the thirties and forties. He is still actively engaged in denominational work. Whether we like it or not, fewer people would know about Cliff Temple, were not J. Earl Mead a part of us. Of course, he still serves on many committees and programs of the Dallas Baptist Association and is Vice Moderator of the Association. This in itself is an honor seldom afforded anyone other than a pastor. He also serves presently as Secretary of the Corporation for the Baptist General Convention of Texas; this is a position he has held for many years. And in 1957 at the meeting of the Southern Baptist Convention in Chicago, he was elected a member of the Southern Baptist Sunday School Board.

But with all these statistics, perhaps the greatest tribute to J. Earl Mead, the Denominational Leader, can come only from one who has served with him through the years. The incomparable J. M. Price says, "Southern Baptists have had a notable line of educational directors including such men as Walter Jackson, Harry Wootan, G. S. Hopkins, Bob Coleman, Clarence Leavell, and Dr. Broughton. In that entire galaxy of notable men, no one has stood out more prominently than Earl Mead.

"For years he has served in his capacity at Cliff Temple, and the remarkable development of that church in the field of religious education has been largely due to his vision, planning, and untiring effort. No one in the South has done a more notable job.

"Likewise he has made distinctive contributions through participation in state and southwide conventions in this field. He served effectively on the committee on correlation of the Southern Baptist Convention. And he has been a leader in and President of the Southwestern Baptist Religious Education Association.

"One of the secrets of his success is his consecration. His life has been an example of what he has sought to get others to be. Recently he gave a series of devotional addresses at the Southwestern Baptist Religious Education meeting and they were the highlight of the meeting. He lives what he teaches.

"Another thing has been his optimistic spirit. He never sounds a low note. People follow a person who believes what he says and knows where he is going. He radiates enthusiasm and courage wherever he goes. And he is a true friend to everyone who knows him.

"And also he is a hard worker. He does not assign work to others to relieve himself of the burden. He bears his part of the burden always and goes through organizational planning, visitation, and personal work. Only eternity will reveal the marvelous results of his remarkable life and service."

Here in a few commanding paragraphs is summarized the philosophy of a life; here is given a yardstick by which values have been measured. The philosophy and measurements are such as to command the attention of one who would hope to succeed as a Christian leader.

November 21, 1958

And There Was Darkness

Just as surely as night follows day in God's pattern for the universe, the dark threads of experience always mingle with the bright ones to complete the divine scheme of the Master Weaver. It seems that we have no more than reached the tops of our mountains to view the vistas before us, until we are once again closed in tightly by the valleys of life.

J. Earl Mead's home was a happy, hilarious, and joy-filled place. When Lois Maxine was just a child, Earl would often play her simple little childish games in order to have fellowship with her. Then, when she became a teenager, he would challenge her in a game of tennis. Often Alice would suggest that he give "Babe" an opportunity to whip him in a game now and then. But this was not for Earl. "Why," he said, "if I threw the game, she would know it in a minute. What she gets in life is going to be the result of achievement." This was the philosophy on which she grew to womanhood.

Many were the times when friends were in the home of the J. Earl Meads. All who know him are aware that Earl has made many friends and close friends wherever he has been in life. From these experiences, many happy memories have come to fill the treasure chest of events in the life of this family. "Almost as though it happened yesterday," says Lois Maxine, "I can hear Daddy stumbling down the hall scattering pots and pans to awaken some visitor who had been our house guest for the night." He has always been an early riser and has a deep conviction that those who sleep away the early hours of the day are missing some of the most beautiful experiences which can be had with the Almighty.

When his daughter entered college in Denton, Texas, J. Earl Mead continued to play the part of her brother, sister, and father. When he would go for Babe at the week's end so that she might spend a few hours at home, they would seldom take the most direct route from Denton to Dallas. Rather they would usually take some back route, where, in a meandering fashion, they could pause to look at the flowers and birds and discuss the problems of living. It is this type of unhurried interest which has caused J. Earl Mead to excel at counseling in his home and in the homes of others.

Thus did J. Earl Mead travel along in a big and busy sea of service until the late spring of 1948. Then, a chain of events began to transpire which seemed to signal the end of a useful, happy, and outstanding career! First, J. Earl Mead lost his voice, and the doctors despaired of his ever speaking again. Then, as though that were not enough, tragedy struck again! Alice had contracted asthma some four or five years previous to this date and it had begun to wear her body down even more than was imagined. On the morning of July 6, 1948, she went to visit a neighbor, but never returned home. While on this visit, she had a cerebral hemorrhage and died in the middle of the afternoon. "ALONE" was the only word which could describe the feeling of the Minister of Education of the Cliff Temple Baptist Church.

At the time, Dr. Bassett was just recovering from surgery. Since the pastor had burdens of his own, Earl Mead hesitated about bothering him about his own health. But now he must send an emissary to see the preacher. At the time, Mr. Mead did not realize that Dr. Bassett's family had to force him to remain in bed to keep him from going to the side of his Minister of Education. The committee was charged with the responsibility of telling the pastor that Mr. Mead was through! He would never speak again! And now, to add to his burdens, his wife had left him for her heavenly home.

When the committee had finished their say, great tears swelled in the eyes of the bulky frame lying upon the bed. And then, slowly, then more surely, the message of reply came. "You go back and tell J. Earl Mead that he has a place of service at Cliff Temple Baptist Church as long as Wallace Bassett has a place. And tell him, further, that I had rather have him without a voice than any other education man in the Southern Baptist Convention with a voice."

This was the only kind of tonic any man would need to bounce back from the "ropes" of defeat. Earl Mead soon began to plan his programs of work for the church. And, to overcome his loss of speech, he would write his speeches and let his assembled workers read them together. During the year in which he had to operate in this fashion, there was a show of loyalty on the part of his workers which has seldom been equaled in any organization. Let us share the first of those speeches, one which appeared on the front page of the *Baptist Standard*.

"The day has arrived, the hour now strikes and God begins to gently but surely draw the curtain which reveals the stage upon which we are to play our particular roles in the coming year. Are you ready? Am I ready? Not if there is something wrong between me and God. Not if anything is wrong between me and anybody else in the whole wide world. Not if my work holds little attraction for me. Not if I have to be compelled from without instead of being impelled from within.

"There is nothing we face between this milestone and our next that can deter or harm us, not even sorrow or death. There is nothing we face but victory if things are right in our hearts. The Lord is Master of all and over all. So we put our hands in His and join hands together then face the future in confidence as our hearts strike up God's song for the journey.

"How I have yearned to make one speech as we begin our fall's work. I got my subject for tonight from the book, *The Bishop's Mantle*. In it, the preacher is musing about a wedding and thinking these words: 'He had officiated at many weddings, but never one, he was thinking, which so pleased him as this one now. Joe's responses were firm in his rich old-country voice; Mary's were clear and sweet. He had been wrong about the years of drab living. There might be luxury or even much comfort. There might always be the pinchpenny hardships. But there would also be love's renewal.'

"Love's renewal was a message for me this summer, as I attempted to recuperate back in God's hills. With the dawn of each morning, I was out with my binoculars, tramping the trails, eyes and ears keenly alerted for God's sights and sounds. Like the morning dew which refreshed the earth, I prayed for the Dew of Heaven to bring renewal to my spirit. The rising sun, the gentle wind, the blue sky, the rippling water, the birds' musical choruses, and all things spoke to me of Love's Renewal. It was love's renewal for Elijah after Carmel which sent him back to God's work. It was love's renewal for Jacob when he wrestled with the angel at Jabbok. It was love's renewal for Peter when he had breakfast with the risen Lord.

Then I remembered what the Lord had said to the church at Ephesus, 'I have somewhat against thee because thou hast left thy first love.'

"So while resting in the hills last summer with Alice seeking relief from asthma, and I the return of my voice, I earnestly prayed, 'Give me love's renewal, O God; renewal and refreshment for the work Thou hast ordained for me to do. Amen!' And now, without voice to make my speech, and without gentle Alice's wise daily counsel, I know I shall find His burden easy and His yoke light since He has given me a renewal of love for the journey. Have you experienced love's renewal for what lies ahead for you?"

November 28, 1958

A Rediscovery of Happiness

In this last chapter in the series to appear in our paper, we are going to let Mrs. Lois Mead tell her own story:

"People are often disillusioned with individuals after knowing them well. But this is not the case with my 'Mister.' I, like many others, hold Mr. Mead on a pedestal as our Christian leader. One day, many years ago now, after the loss of my husband, Mr. Mead and Dr. Bassett approached me about becoming church visitor. This was quite a shock to me as I did not know they were seeking such a worker, much less that they would consider me for the job.

"On November 1, 1944, I started working for Cliff Temple, having as my boss, Mr. J. Earl Mead. I felt very close to the Mead family and very often visited Alice and ran errands for her. One time in particular, I remember when the grandson, Mead, got sick, and Mr. Mead was away from home. Babe and I had to put Mead in the hospital. He had mononucleosis. I'll never forget that disease, for I had such a difficult time learning to pronounce it. That was a very critical time for the family.

"I was in Houston at the time of Alice's death. I tried to console Mr. Mead in his sorrow because of Alice's homegoing, having gone through the excruciating experience of giving up a mate only a short time previous.

"Time and work are great healers of the tragic hurts which pierce the human heart. Mr. Mead worked hard at the job of continuing in his service for Cliff Temple, but it was obvious to all of us that he was lonely. Much later he told me of his feeling toward me. This I could not fathom because of his position and his wonderful abilities. I could not see how he could take even a second look at me, a very insignificant person who was working for him. I was never so shocked in my life. I went home, telling no one, of course. But that afternoon my yard got a good soaking. I squirted water from the hose on all the flowers, shrubs, and grass; I would cry then laugh, saying to myself, 'This could not happen to me, as many wonderful people as he knows, to ever care for me.' Yet I knew that he was sincere and never a hypocrite; and I knew he would never 'string me along.' I thought it too wonderful to be true, and dared not let myself believe it.

"Needless to say, this love grew and grew. He kept me so spellbound in our courtship that one day he said, 'Why don't you say something?' I replied that all I had thought he could do was run a Sunday School. Should he ever write a book on 'How to Woo and Win a Widow,' he would make a million. A volume could be written on our courtship: on how he courted my daughter, on how we had to divide our times together, sandwiching them between meetings and speeches.

"In July 1949 he met Betty Lois, my daughter, and me at my parent's home in Weslaco. He wanted to tell them himself about our love, as if they hadn't already suspected it. He came on the train from Dallas to Edinburg, getting there at a very early hour. We were to drive over from Weslaco to meet him. My father insisted on Betty Lois not getting up so early to go with me to meet Mr. Mead, but she felt as if he was coming to see her as much as to see me, and she went with me. It was hard ever to be alone with him, because Betty Lois loved him and wanted to be with him, too.

"Betty Lois was a challenge to J. Earl Mead. Loving people as he does, he immediately wanted to furnish her with the loving kindness that had been taken from her with the loss of her father. But she was a quiet and a sometimes difficult to approach person. But he won her completely. And, in fact, she recently said of him, 'I have just never felt 'step.' He is our father, father-in-law, and grandfather, and we dearly love him.'

"On October 19, 1949, my father performed the wedding ceremony in his home at Weslaco. We spent a part of our honeymoon in Kerrville, and several very funny things happened there. Mr. Mead almost ran off with the wrong woman one night when he took her arm to help her from the elevator, thinking he had hold of my arm.

"We visited Mr. Mead's father in Wakita, Oklahoma, and returned home. The church gave us a very wonderful reception, presenting us with a beautiful silver service which we prize very highly. Mr. Mead's family and friends took me in, because they wanted him to be happy. On one visit to Missouri and his old home, one of his cousins invited us to be her guests. Now cousin Gertie was a 'little leary' about second marriages and she had more or less made up her mind that she wasn't going to care for me particularly. But upon our making ready to leave, she said, after embracing me, 'Lois, I just love you better than I aimed to.' That spoke volumes to me, and Gertie and I have been the best of pals ever since.

" 'The Mister' and I have made many, many trips together, always taking a roadside picnic lunch along, even if leaving around noon. Our trips are always most enjoyable, going to banquet speeches, study courses, visiting relatives, vacationing, etc. I have learned a lot about birds and flowers since marrying him. The only bird I had known was a 'chee-chee' before he introduced me to a dickcissel, painted bunting, and many others. He is always interested in nature around him and makes one have a deep appreciation for the commonplace things of life.

"What an inspiration to follow him around, and that is exactly what I do, and about all I do. I feel just as much a call of God to take care of Mr. Mead as I would to be in some special Christian service. I feel so inadequate myself, but I have thought if I could keep him well and happy, that I would have a part in the good he does.

"My 'Mister' is very easy to please. He is everything his followers think him to be and much more. And since I have known him as a Christian leader, as a boss, and as a husband, I can say he is the best Christian I have ever known, and more wonderful than anyone can imagine.

"I have said so many times: 'There is not another in the world. He has the power to inspire unmatched anywhere. Volumes could be written about the people he has inspired to go into special service. He cannot be surpassed in his consoling words to bereaved families.'

"I wouldn't trade him off for a million."

And so, in this new found joy of the life and service of J. Earl Mead, he continues to serve. And may it so be for many more blessed years.
---John C. Shanks, 1958

The A. C. Mead family circa 1896. From left to right are Wilma Mattie, Alvin Callaway, James Earl, Zora Ina and Vida Amanda Smith Mead.

J. Earl Mead's boyhood home near Fair Play, Missouri

Earl Mead at Bismont Baptist Church located near Fair Play, Missouri

John Caswell Smith, Earl's maternal grandfather, seated in the
legislative chambers of the State of Oklahoma in 1915

The J. Earl Mead family in 1917: Alice, Lois Maxine and Earl

The first home of J. Earl and Alice Lenora
Groom Mead in Wakita, Oklahoma

The J. Earl Mead family, circa 1919

First Baptist Church in Beaumont, Texas

Pictured above are Alice and Earl Mead on an outing in Beaumont.

Pictured outside their home in Dallas, Texas,
are Alice and Earl in the mid-1940s.

The Cliff Temple Baptist Church staff circa 1952. Seated behind the
desk from left to right are J. Earl Mead, Dr. Wallace Bassett and J. B.
Christian. Standing behind them are Brittie Stinson, Virginia Goslin,
Louie McNamara, John Shanks, Gerry Mansfield and Lois Riddle Mead.

J. Earl Mead speaking at a banquet given in his
honor in Shreveport, Louisiana in 1958

Lois and Earl Mead in the kitchen of their Dallas
home enjoying a playful moment in 1956

Earl Mead with the three "Loises" in his life in the early
1960s. Left to right are Earl, Lois Maxine Mead Johnson,
Lois Riddle Mead and Betty Lois Harper McGee.

Alvin Callaway Mead is pictured above on the left seated
next to his son, Earl Mead in the early 1960s

Mr. Mead, as seen above, is speaking to his audience at dawn
in the Prayer Garden at Glorieta in the early 1960s.

Earl Mead speaking at Glorieta

This rugged stone pulpit, which was built as a memorial to J. Earl Mead, stands in The Prayer Garden at Glorieta Conference Center (formerly known as Glorieta Baptist Assembly) near Santa Fe, New Mexico. It was dedicated to the memory of Mr. Mead on September 22, 1988. We give special recognition and thanks to Mike Goff of the Glorieta Conference Center for his willing attitude and diligent research in discovering this precise date for our publication.

Earl Mead, observing the heights, up Glorieta canyon

Lois and Earl Mead in the 1970s

J. Earl and Lois Mead celebrating his ninety-fifth birthday at John Knox Lake Forest Village in Denton, Texas in April, 1987

Part II

My Life Story

Written by J. Earl Mead
1978

Introduction

Many times in the past, I tried to introduce J. Earl Mead in a way that would be adequate to address the greatness of the man, and, at the same time, attempt to conceal my extreme bias! He was like a second father to me. I never felt toward another "boss" as I felt toward this man. I wish all could have known him as I came to know him!

What a story! He came from a one-room log cabin to become a spiritual giant, recognized across America as "Mr. Education Director." But let him tell you the whole story in his own words and in his own style, as we asked him to do many years ago.

John. C. Shanks, PhD.

Boyhood in the Ozarks

I was born, James Earl Mead, April 27, 1892, in a one-room log cabin on the banks of Barren Creek, three miles east of Fairplay, Polk County, Missouri. My father was Alvin Callaway Mead, the son of James Madison Mead and Nancy Ann (Hash) Mead. My mother Vida Amanda Mead was the daughter of John Caswell Smith, called "Uncle Polk," and Margaret Elander (Thompson) Smith.

This put my birthplace in the foothills of the Ozarks. It was a timbered, rocky country of spring-fed streams, timothy and clover meadows and orchards. There were walnut and hickory nut trees. Wild blackberries and dewberry vines were strewn along the winding roads and at the margin of the forests. As a lad I had many an excursion for this wild fruit, and for blackhaws, may apples, hazelnuts and persimmons. It was in this outdoor environment that I got my love for nature. I became a student of the birds, wild flowers, trees, shrubs, and vines.

In speaking of my birth, I often tell of winning my first race with Father. It was on this wise: On the day of my birth, Father was plowing in the field. Knowing the birth of a child was imminent, Father arranged with Mother to hang a white sheet on the line if she felt the pains of coming birth. In the course of the morning, as Father came to the end of a row and turned his horse, he saw the white sheet waving on the line. Hurriedly he unhitched his horse and went to the house, checked with Mother, then mounted his horse and trotted away to the village to get the doctor. (It must be remembered we had no telephones in that community in those days.) As Father passed Grandmother's home, he stopped to inform her of the approaching birth. Grandmother hurried over to be with Mother. In due time, Father and Dr. Hopkins arrived, but not until after I had been born. So I always tell this story of my birth and add, "I beat my father in our first race."

There was a sister Zora Ina, who was my senior by about two years. Three years after my birth, the last child Wilma Mattie was born. So there were three Mead kids, and we survive until this day (January 13, 1978). Both sisters, widowed now, live in Caldwell, Kansas, each in her own home. The three of us have semi-annual visits, and these meetings are among the most cherished experiences of my life.

Both Grandfather Smith and Grandfather Mead were Union soldiers in the War Between the States. Grandfather Smith used to regale us grandchildren with hair-raising stories of his battles and experiences during the war. We lived along the line which divided the North from the South. Though my grandfathers fought on the Union side, my great-grandfather, James Thompson, owned slaves. When the ravages of war drew near, my great-grandfather went, with his slaves, to Dallas, Texas, to leave them with relatives until the trouble was over. It was his intention to return to Polk County, but he died near Dallas in the fall of 1866. His body lies in the old Horton Cemetery north of Arcadia, Texas. I have been to this old neglected cemetery several times trying to locate James Thompson's grave, but the markers are all gone or broken up, and my search was in vain.

On my Grandmother Smith's side I can trace my lineage back to the Revolutionary War, and have been to the grave of my great-great-great-grandfather, James Hopkins, who fought in that war. He was buried in the cemetery near the cave spring in the western part of Polk County, west of Fair Play.

Most of those living in the community of my birth were relatives of mine. I remember all four of my grandparents, a great-grandmother, and many great-uncles and great-aunts, and still a larger number of uncles and aunts. There were forty-two of us cousins on father's side alone. I sometimes say, "About the best crop we could raise in those rocky hills was children."

I moved in and out among these kinsmen to my heart's delight. We all lived within four miles of each other. Often we gathered at Grandmother Mead's for Sunday dinner. I often wonder, since I am older, how Grandmother found enough food on the table to feed us all.

We moved from the log cabin down by the creek to our new house, a mile north. It was situated on a hill above the Mead grandparents. I thought we had ample quarters in the new house, but later, when I counted them, there were only two rooms with a smoke house and a henhouse nearby. The tiled well from which I regularly drew water in the long tin bucket which hung on a peg at the well, was situated on the porch. The thing best remembered in this move was the barn raising. On that day all our neighbors came to help drag the felled logs to the site, and lifted them and put them in their proper places. These long, heavy logs were cut from the timber on our land. There was the big spread at mealtime which no one could ever forget.

In my mind also were the home made carpets which were laid on the floors. We put straw on the wooden floors for matting, and then stretched the carpet on the best we could, and tacked it along the walls. The lane to Grandpa's was forested. When I went on errands at night time to get something at Grandpa's, I would run as fast as my legs would carry me, imagining a ghost behind every tree and an owl on every limb. It seemed to me I barely escaped being nabbed by these as I raced home and shut the door.

There was little money in any hands in our community in those days. About all we had to buy was coffee and sugar. We raised our hogs and chickens. Hog killing time in the fall was exciting. We would build a fire, and throw flint rocks in it. When the rocks got hot they would be lifted and put in the water in the tilted barrel until the water was hot enough for the scalding of the hogs. Salting, smoking and curing the meat followed. We ate little beef for there was no refrigeration with which to preserve the meat. We had plenty of chickens and eggs and bacon and ham. As the saying was, "We lived high off the hog."

We had our own orchards and gardens which kept us in fruit and vegetables. Father would sit astride his horse, as a lad, with a sack of corn or wheat across the back of the saddle and go to mill. There the miller would grind the grain, take his toll, and tie the sack and return it to the horse's back and Father would be on his way home with his meal or flour.

I had no idea we were poor in those days, for we were about as well off as all our neighbors. Long afterwards, when Father was wintering in our home, as his custom was (I preached his funeral after he was 99 years of age), I asked at table, "Father, in which bank did you keep your money when I was a boy?" He chuckled and replied, "Why, Earl, I didn't have any money." As I have said, I did not know we were poor, but I know we ate lots of milk and mush. I like that tasty mixture to this good day.

Church was always a big part of my life. When I was a mere lad in the Ozarks, we would walk a mile to the old country church of which my grandmother was a charter member. This dear church, Bismont, was located on Uncle Tom Mead's farm. He had deeded the church two acres from the corner of his land. Cousin Minnie Mead taught my Sunday School Class, which was called the Card Class.

Father led the music in the little church. I have a mental picture of Father to this day sitting at home with a tuning fork in hand, "sol-fa-la-ing" the new songs so as to be ready for the following Sunday's services. In that church, which meant so much to me in my boyhood, I remember revivals and conversions. When Cousin Connie Mead was converted, his mother, Aunt Aggie, shouted up and down the aisles in joy and happiness.

There was a great-grandmother, Mary Ann Thompson, whose husband, as I have already related, died near Dallas, Texas. I can see her now sitting by the fireside, lighting her clay pipe with embers from the fireplace. I remember her, too, sitting in the rocking chair on the porch with her black slat sunbonnet on her head, as she chattered with her friends.

Our lives were fairly simple, and our world went no farther than our valley. How narrow were our horizons! We had no telephones. There were no electric lights. My boyhood job was to fill the coal oil lamps, trim the wicks and keep the smoked chimneys clean. Too, I kept the woodbox back of the stove filled with suitable wood. It seemed to me that the woodbox was always empty. Mother encouraged me in my wood carrying chores. She would say, "Son, you are the smartest boy I have. Will you bring in an arm load of wood?" I thought she was speaking of the three of us children. It did not occur to me that I was the only boy, until after I had acquired the habit of carrying in wood.

There was the old one-room one-teacher country schoolhouse. There I studied my spelling lessons well that I might earn the coveted head mark and go to the head of the line. The school was called the Pickle School for it was on Mr. Pickle's land. On the hill above the schoolhouse lived Uncle Columbus and Aunt Callie Hopkins. I felt fortunate if I were chosen as one to go up the hill and fetch a pail of water. Outside school terms I had a wonderful time with this family, for there were twelve children there. We could play most any game and have enough for two sides with some still on the bench.

Though I was too young to do heavy farming work like plowing or stacking wheat, there were other family chores to keep me busy. I remember my pastor Wallace Bassett saying fifty years later that, "The city has nothing to discipline children like the old country chores." My chores included the feeding of the chickens, gathering the eggs, going to the pasture for the cows, planting corn by hand, hoeing the garden and running errands for my parents.

Once, through the planting of corn, my father taught me a very valuable lesson. My cousin and I were dropping corn from our empty syrup buckets in the places designated by the crossing of Father's checked furrows. In the afternoon, when we were tired and anxious for the day to end, Father left his horse and plows and came across the field. He looked into our buckets and said, "Boys, when you have planted all the corn in your buckets you may go home." Father left and we trudged on. Although my cousin had about the same amount of corn in his bucket as I, when I looked around, he was crawling over the fence and heading for home. About three weeks later, when this cousin came to visit us, Father said, "Boys, let's go up and see the corn you planted." To the field we went. Father led us to a place where hundreds of little green slips of corn had sprouted and come up in an eight- or ten-foot space. No sooner did my cousin see that than he began to cry and headed for the fence, for he remembered when he turned his bucket upside down and got rid of all his corn at once. The valuable lesson I learned was "Be sure your sins will find you out."

Another lesson Mother drilled into my mind: If I tarried to do any work she assigned me, she would tell about the lazy man who would not work. He was told, "Unless you work we will have to haul you off to the poorhouse." In spite of that threat, he failed to work. So they loaded the lazy man into a wagon and started for the poorhouse. As they drove along, passersby came up and heard the story and offered to help. One came by and offered the lazy man some corn. He rose up in the wagon and asked, "Is it shelled?" "No," they replied. "Then drive on," the lazy man said. Often if I showed signs of being lazy, Mother's story sent me back to my work again.

There is no memory more nostalgic than our fishing trips. The whole community would go. We would hitch our horses to the wagons and drive to the rivers for a day or two of seining, which was lawful in those days. These pleasurable times, with great fish fries, and good fun together often return to my memory.

Visits to families of my cousins brought much happiness. Once my parents hitched the horses to the hack, which is a two-seated buggy without a top, and we set out to see cousins Forrest and Clarice Hale. Their mother was my mother's sister. I was riding on the back seat by myself as we started up a steep rocky hill. The seat turned backwards and I fell on the ground behind the hack, seat and all. It was not until Father got to the top of the hill that the accident was discovered and they came back for me.

When heavy snows would fall, Father would hitch the old mule to a big log and drag it along the road to make a path to school for us.

The old Pickle School is etched on my mind. It was a two-mile trek from home. On the way a number of cousins joined us in our walk. We would take our lunches along, and I considered a baked sweet potato about the best morsel of food when eating time came. In cold weather, as we gathered around the stove, the strong odor of asafetida greeted our nostrils. Mother never tied that smelly stuff around our necks, but many children wore it around their necks to ward off colds and other diseases.

When frosts would come, it was then we always stopped under persimmon trees on our way home to sate our appetites with this luscious fruit. One day at school the girl I "claimed" as a sweetheart, because of some infraction of the school rules, was made to sit on the teacher's desk and eat an apple in front of the whole school. How I suffered! I felt the whole world was aware of her disgrace.

There was Grandfather's orchard. In the springtime the whole orchard was white and pink with blossoms and their fragrance can never be forgotten. It seemed to us boys that the apples would never get ripe. We often rushed the season by picking green apples, and eating them, but the resultant stomachaches soon put a stop to that. But we found a way to eat these apples without having stomachaches. We would pull the apples and take them down to the ever-flowing spring of cold, pure water that bubbled up from under the red oak at the bottom of the hill beyond Grandpa's barn. There we put the apples in the spring and they would be rolled and bumped over the rocks at the bottom of the stream until they were bruised and brown. We would run through the clover field, down beyond the water-gap, and pick up the apples. They were not yet ripe, but tasty, and the stomachache was gone.

There was also the time cousins climbed a wild cherry tree the day we visited Uncle Fred's and Aunt Mollie's. As I think of it now, I was never sicker in my life than after eating too many wild cherries.

Once sister Zora and I went to the pasture to climb hickory trees and fill our baskets with nuts. Grandpa's old rams kept us up those trees for a long time before they wandered away. Then Zora and I raced for the fence, arriving safely. When a neighbor's dogs got into Grandfather's flock of sheep, killing some and wounding others, it left a sad memory in the mind of this little boy who went to view the disaster.

I learned a lesson about exaggeration from Mother. (Many good lessons we learn from our fathers and mothers.) I had been wandering around in the woods and came to an open glade and found some wild strawberries. I raced home and begged Mother to come and we would gather wild strawberries. Mother questioned me about how many strawberries there were. "A whole field of them," I answered. Mother told me she was tired, but upon my insistence she joined me. The story does not turn out very well. It was a long journey for a tired mother. When we got to the field, there were very few berries to be found. I went home crest-fallen and sorry. For me it was a good lesson in not stretching the truth.

We made our own soap. There was the ash hopper where we deposited the residue from the fireplace. Water would be poured into the hopper with a bucket on a spout below to catch the drip. Afterwards, in a black pot over the outside fire, soap would be made and set out to dry and then cut in squares.

Grandmother always kept geese. Often in the winter time I have seen her with her apron on, a goose on its back in her lap, with its head held under her arm, as she plucked the down from the breast of the goose with which to make soft feather beds and pillows. When snows used to come, Mother would describe it as "the old woman picking her geese."

We lived only seven miles from the county seat, Bolivar, and though I was ten years old when we left the Ozarks, I was only at Bolivar twice. With horse pulled wagons, buggies, and hacks, we did not get very far away from home. Though a very small world was mine, it was a pleasant and happy world, among my kinsmen, and the memories of those boyhood days are among the most cherished of my life.

I learned many lessons which have served me well in life. There was the time Father and I were harvesting potatoes by the side of the road. As we labored, we heard the sound of steel rims rolling over the flint stones. We heard the wagon long before it and the driver came into view. When the neighbor came near to where we were, he said, "Whoa," and reined his horses to a stop. Then he called to Father, "Callaway, how are your taters turnin' out?" I shall never forget Father's reply. He got to his feet, brushed the soil from his hands, and shouted, "They're not turnin' out at all. We're having to dig 'em out." What a lesson to learn about industry.

In the winter there was trapping. It was fun to run traps on snowy days to see if they held any game. Uncle Will and I went together to make the rounds of his traps. As we advanced we saw a trap was sprung. Uncle Will put his hand under the trap carefully and retrieved a cottontail rabbit. He held it up and then the rabbit twisted itself from Uncle's hand and ran away. As it disappeared in the snow and grass, Uncle sadly exclaimed, "There goes a nickel!"

Those first years of my life are among my happiest memories. Those years were full of school, church, kinsmen, chores, and fun. I thank my godly father and saintly mother for the sweet nest of home for my beginning.

As an appendage to this Ozark tale let me add this: Mother would call for dinner, and I would come rushing from outdoors, always ready to eat. I would rush to the table and sit down, and then would come Mother's inquiry, "Son, have you washed?" Never could I eat until I had washed. I think it is just an example of our work for the Lord. One needs to have a clean heart to be allowed the bounties at His table.

Growing Up
In the Cherokee Strip

I was ten years old when we left the Ozark country to reside in the new Cherokee Strip of northwestern Oklahoma. Our move was necessitated because of Grandmother Smith's worsening asthma. I remember, when on more than one occasion, I heard the sound of a horse's hoofs on the rocky lane, as Uncle Will came on horseback to shout out, "Come quickly; Mother is dying!" Grandmother had long suffered from asthma. The doctor told Grandfather and the family, after one of Grandmother's asthma attacks, "Mrs. Smith must be taken to a dryer climate. She cannot live here." So it came about that Grandfather and my father went westward to seek out a suitable place for Grandmother's health.

Land was purchased in northwestern Oklahoma. The strip of land south of the Kansas border was opened for settlement in 1893. Our family arrived there around the first of February 1903, just ten years after the Cherokee Strip was opened for settlement. Other families than ours moved also. It took an entire passenger coach to hold the migrants.

What a strange and different country for a ten-year-old boy. There were no trees. There were only stretches of prairie land as far as the eye could see. This land was covered with tall blue stem grass. Much of the soil had never been tilled. No more did we see clear bubbling springs and fast flowing, singing streams. All streams had winding, dirty ribbons of water running through beds of mud. There was little beauty about the creeks and rivers.

There was the stiff wind and the rolling dust which bothered and plagued us. We had never been conscious of winds in the timbered country we had left. We often left our house for the cellar when we saw a black cloud of dust rolling in, being pushed by the wind.

Here again was the one-room, one-teacher school house. It was a country school two and a half miles from where we lived. One winter I rode to school in a buggy with my teacher, John Rackley. It cost me nothing, for I would wait down the road with a bundle of oats in my hand for his horse.

There was another thing which was different from the Ozarks. Back in Missouri we had clear, pure, cold water to drink from deep wells or springs. Now we had gypsum water from shallow wells. Both its odor and taste made it difficult to drink. Later we dug our own cistern and lined it with cement. We caught rain water from the eaves of the house and filtered it through charcoal. It was much better than gypsum water, but never as cool and refreshing as our Missouri water.

We raised wheat on the farm for the most part. I was now old enough to take part in the work of the field. Wheat harvest time found me gathering and stacking bundles into shocks. In the Ozarks the shock was always topped by two bundles of broken straw, called the capsheaf, to shed the rainfall, but in our new country this capsheaf was not needed because the rainfall was light.

At corn harvest time, I was assigned to take the down row, which is the row broken down as the wagon passed over it. I became acquainted for the first time with alfalfa. We mowed the field three or four times in a season. We sold some of the crop, but hauled most of it to the red barn which had been built for that purpose. We fed this to the cattle during the winter. I can yet see, in my mind's eye, the large letters on the end of the barn: "A L F A L F A."

It was now my daily stint to milk the cows morning and night. It seems to me, now that I think of it, those cows were always at the back side of the pasture at milking time, and I would have to drive them in. I have always said, "I never liked to milk in fly time or in cold weather." That, of course, means I did not relish milking at any time at all. In fly time, the old cow was sure to swish her tail and brush my face, or kick over the bucket. In cold weather, my hands became numb with the weather. But milk was a necessity, so I never got away from that chore. Later, when we moved to town, added to the milking, was added the task of leading the cow to a vacant lot lush with grass, and staking her out every morning, and returning for her every evening.

74

Hunting plovers came in the summer time. Grandfather would hitch old Jim to the buggy and we would drive to the pasture. He carried the gun and I drove old Jim. We lived mostly on plover and plover gravy that first summer. That is a tasty dish. In those days we could always get enough plovers for a mess for the family. Killing plovers has long been outlawed. I remember my last plover hunt, when I handled the gun. I got forty-one plovers with forty-two shots.

The first winter, after our arrival in the Cherokee Strip, a railroad was being built. It passed near where we lived. That was a very interesting winter, for I often watched the workmen with their horses, equipment, and tools grading, laying ties, and driving spikes to hold the rails in place.

I must not forget to report that the move to Oklahoma cured Grandmother's asthma, and she lived to a ripe old age. We were all grateful to God for her cure.

After two years on the farm we moved to Carmen, Oklahoma, a few miles away. There I completed my elementary and high school education. The high school only included the tenth grade. Father and Grandfather opened the Smith and Mead Produce Company. They bought poultry and eggs from the farmers and sold these products wholesale.

At school I became proficient in spelling; in fact, I was named the best speller in our school, so was chosen to represent the school in county competition. I remember the long evenings I spent with the principal, cramming for that contest. He gave out long five- and six-syllable words from the physiology glossary as practice. I was well prepared for the county contest. It was an oral affair, and always being a timid boy, I was very nervous and ill at ease on my feet. They gave me the word sweat. Young Earl spelled it – "s-w-e-t, sweat," and went down ignominiously. Come to think of it, there were only five in the high school graduating class. But graduation was a big event for the school, the village, and especially for us five graduates.

Sunday School and church going continued to be an important part of my life. Mother and Father always went to church and took their children with them. Toward the end of Father's life, as he sat at our table, I said, "Father, I want to thank you for putting the church in my life for it has been the center around which my life has revolved." At the time I spoke thus to my father, I had spent over half a century devoting myself to serving churches as Minister of Education.

I was converted in the time of revival in the Carmen Baptist Church in the fall of 1911. That means I was nineteen years old before I trusted the

Lord as my Savior. Why the delay I cannot explain, for my parents were devout and godly people. During that revival week I felt a deep conviction for my sins, and my lost condition bore me down. I remember those awful days and nights of suffering. I felt I was all alone in my misery, and although my parents slept in a bedroom across the living room from where I slept, I felt I was far away and all alone. Oh, the anguish and suffering of those days!

One night at church following the sermon, the evangelist gave the invitation for people to accept Christ as a personal Savior. I was struggling to find decision and peace. I do not know how it would have turned out, had not my sister come and put her arms around me, and with tears urged me to give my heart to Jesus. That did it! I moved forward, grasped the preacher by the hand, and took my seat. Joy filled my soul. I had become a Christian. I consider this the greatest decision I ever made in my life.

Pastor John L. Bandy baptized me on October 10, 1911. Soon thereafter Brother Bandy set me to work serving the Lord as choir director and song leader for the church. One never forgets the person who puts him to his first Christian work. Forty years later, when Cliff Temple Baptist Church, Dallas, wanted me to write my life's story, the church sent John Shanks with Mrs. Mead and me to retrace my steps. The first place we visited was five hundred miles away to see this pastor who gave me a start in Christian service. I had held him in high esteem all my life. I feel it was the opening door to a life's work for the Lord.

Those were pleasant, happy growing-up days at Carmen. My first work for pay was building fires and sweeping out the bank. In the summer time I earned some money tending lawns. There was the stint of clerking at Jim's and John's general store. There, besides inside work, I made the rounds soliciting grocery orders, and later in the day delivering them. Building egg cases for Father's firm added some to my meager earnings.

In my last Carmen year, Thomas S. Cobb and a Mr. Holtzclaw held a music school in our church. I followed them to other schools and taught some. A term at a music school in Fort Worth followed. There we studied sight reading, harmony, counterpoint and directing. Nor can I forget the summer that followed when I donned a derby, fancy suit, turned-back collar and a cravat, put a baton in my hand and went afield in Texas teaching my own music schools in churches. In the fall of 1911 our family moved to Wakita, Oklahoma, where Father established a firm called The Wakita Produce Company.

I lived in Wakita for eight years. Wakita was a small village of 300 residents. The town was located in the wheat country. If there is a scene more beautiful in the springtime than the wheat country, I have never seen it. When the wheat heads in the spring and bends with the wind, it makes a never-to-be forgotten sight. Then come the golden days of harvest time. Those sights will remain forever etched in memory.

Soon after our arrival in Wakita, Mother and I were quarantined with the smallpox which was the scourge of the community that fall. Father and Wilma had to stay away from home until Mother and I got well and the quarantine was lifted. By now my older sister, Zora had married Oscar Haubold. They lived in Kennewick, Washington.

Being undecided as to what to do in life, I did not go to college after high school graduation in Carmen. This I have always regretted. It was decided I should spend two years in Wichita Business College. This was a delightful and interesting experience and stood me in good stead all my life. Not only did I learn book-keeping, typing, and shorthand, but the teachers themselves left an indelible contribution to my life.

I stood first in rapid calculation in my school and was to have represented my school in national competition, but the contest was never held because of the turmoil of the approaching World War.

After completing my courses in Wichita Business College and graduating, I returned to Wakita, and Father took me in as full partner in his business. Soon he and the family moved to Anthony, Kansas, and opened a like business. I was left to run the Wakita store.

Soon after we moved to Wakita, we built a tennis court by our home. Also we built a tennis court by the church. This brought many young people to our home. My parents always kept an open house where friends were welcome. Since the establishment of my own home, this practice has been continued and has resulted in untold blessings to our family.

On Sundays the young people would go kodaking or walking. There was not much else to do in a small village in those days: there were no radios, no televisions, and no movies. I have very happy memories of those days.

The Wakita Baptist Church had a great influence in my life. My Sunday School teachers, pastors, and leaders in the church made a lasting contribution to my life. Preachers have always been a special group to me. I have spent most of my life on church staffs trying to help them make their dreams come true. I have always hesitated to criticize these men of the cloth. I read in the Bible where children called Elisha an old bald head, and forty-two she-bears came out of the woods and mauled them. If I had something bad to say about a preacher, I have always been afraid of the she-bears and the he-bears also. Thus I have refrained from criticizing them.

I returned to that dear church in Wakita after an absence of fifty-eight years to make a dedicatory talk when the church built an addition and enlarged their church house. I paid a tribute of appreciation to the church and its members for what the church had meant to me. I was aware as I spoke, that the leaders there in my day were now all with the Lord.

I remember the pastors we had. I had close fellowship with them because I was the song leader of the church, a work for which I was never paid, nor did I expect remuneration for it. It was simply my Christian service to the church and congregation. When these pastors came, we would all embrace them in love and be more diligent in service. Usually, as is the case in a small town, pastors scarcely stayed more than two years. They would grow discouraged, or a larger church would call them. I sometimes smilingly say, "These pastors would come with high hopes and tell us from the pulpit how we ought to live. Later we found it easier to change pastors than to change our ways of living."

One pastor, G. S. Jobe, after he knew his church members well, preached a sermon in which he used the heads of families as points in his sermon. I do not remember his text. I thought him to be a brave man to preach such a sermon. Introducing his points, he would say, "There is Ernest Lemon" and "There is Earl Mead" and so on. He mentioned each man's good points, then parading our short comings before the whole congregation. He was not our pastor for long after that. It would have been a fair exchange if Jobe had let one of us add another point; namely, "There is G. S. Jobe," at the end of his sermon.

The church choir which I directed was known all over that community. We were often asked to sing in churches over the county and give special music at associational meetings. I remember the occasion when the choir arose to sing, and while standing, someone raised a window behind the bass section and removed a chair. When the song was over Gordon Neville took his seat, but there was no seat there, and he fell noisily to the floor.

Alice Lenora Groom, who lived with her parents in Winfield, Kansas, came to Wakita to visit her sister and family. Soon I was dating this slender, graceful, attractive young lady. She remained for some months working in a local store. She won my heart, and when she returned home, I would board a train to Winfield on week-ends to pursue my courtship. Alice's parents never let her meet me at the depot, for they thought it improper for a young lady thus to do. When I arrived in Winfield, I would take a horse drawn cab to the Groom residence.

This courtship continued for several months and culminated in a proposal and marriage. We rented a house in Wakita, furnished it and there we were married. John L. Bandy read the ceremony. He was the preacher who had baptized me. I remember well the last thing we took to our new home the evening we were married. It was a butcher knife, which was the source of laughter ever after. The marriage took place on the evening of June 9, 1915.

Our happiness was enhanced by the arrival of Lois Maxine, May 14, 1916. Babe, as we lovingly called her, was to be the greatest blessing of our lives. She was an only child. Always we have been proud of her. Since she was an only child, I was able to play many games with her. When she got to be a young girl, we often played tennis together. She married Malcolm Johnson, and they had three children, Mead, Martha and Margaret. So it was a family of M's: Malcolm, Maxine, Mead, Martha and Margaret.

At the time of our daughter's birth, we almost lost both mother and the baby. "Blood poisoning," the doctors said of the mother. "Undernourishment," they said of the daughter. Their lives hung in the balance for many anxious days. But good doctors, a skilled surgeon, and a dear nurse pulled them through to health and strength again.

Early in 1917 we learned from the doctors that Mother had cancer. This knowledge brought fear and sadness to all our hearts. My parents had moved from Anthony to Caldwell. Mother's physical condition grew gradually worse. When she was no longer strong enough to be up, we often spent as much time as we could at her bedside. It was the summer of 1918 when we lost her. She was buried in the Wakita cemetery.

I must not pass over this tearful experience without relating two matters which had a lasting influence upon my life. The first event was Mother's death itself. For the first time it had been brought home to me that life has an ending here on earth. This fact caused me to check my life to see if I was putting it to the best use. Just before Mother expired, she called me to her bedside. I bent down to hear what she had to say. In her frail, weak voice she said, "Son, will you promise me something?" Though I did not know what she was to ask, I knew I would promise. She continued, "Will you promise me you will always do what God wants you to do?" I promised. I pray I have always kept that promise.

The second event concerns Father. Just before Mother died, he came in from work one day, stopped to kiss Mother, and ask her how she felt.

Then he beckoned me to follow him. We went down the hall, through the kitchen, down the back steps and took seats in the shade of a tree in the back yard. Then Father began, "Earl, I was not converted until after you were born. Soon after my conversion, while plowing in the field, I felt that God asked me to preach. As you know, this I never did." Father stopped talking. His frame began to shake, and as tears rolled down his cheeks, he continued, "Do you think God would spare Mother if I would begin preaching now?" I never looked into the face of a sadder man. He was now past fifty years of age. Father felt he had missed the purpose for which God gave him birth.

These two moving experiences made a deep impression on my life. How earnestly I prayed, "Dear God, don't let me miss the thing for which you brought me into the world."

I had a commitment to lead the music at Falls Creek Baptist Assembly, which date came soon after Mother's death. The whole family thought that date should be kept. Grandfather Smith, Father, Alice and Lois Maxine went with me. That was the second annual meeting of the camp. Most of us lived in tents during the week. The week at Falls Creek helped heal the sorrow of Mother's death and afforded me many hours of pondering over what I was to do with my own life.

A year later, in 1919, I returned to Falls Creek to lead the music. I now come to one of the most decisive moments of my entire life. Reverend A. E. Booth, who had just been called as pastor of the First Baptist Church, Beaumont, Texas, near the Gulf of Mexico, was at Falls Creek to teach a class. After seeing me and watching me in action, he asked for a conference. "Have you ever considered giving your life to God's work?" he asked. "Would you come and help me in my work at Beaumont?" he appealed. "I want to find the will of God and do it," I responded, remembering my promise to Mother on her deathbed.

As I look back now, after half a century, I realize that I became more and more interested in the Lord's business. My deepest satisfactions were coming from my Christian work. I had gone with evangelists to meetings and led the revival music. Once, John L. Bandy came to plead with me to become a life's partner with him in revival work. He was to do the preaching, and I, the song leading. I turned the invitation down, saying, "I do not feel of God to do so."

But at Falls Creek I felt definitely called to give my life to work in the churches. Moses stood by the burning bush. Isaiah felt such a call as he went to worship in the temple. Gideon had his encounter with God down by the threshing floor. It was at Falls Creek I stood by my burning bush and was to make a decision that forever affected my life, and from which I have had untold joy.

Young men have sought me along the way as they considered the question as to what they were to do in life. I have always said, "Do not go into church work unless you feel God's call to do so." It takes this heart-searching experience if one is to stay at it. Many times, when I have felt my inability to meet the responsibilities of my work, I might have returned to the business world had I not felt such a call. And to this day, when I am past eighty, I still "follow the gleam" of God's call into His work.

When I returned home from Falls Creek, I shared my experience with my wife. Babe was only three and was too young to know about such things. Alice encouraged me, and promised whatever my decision it would be her decision also. What a struggle! Long after my family was in bed, I would sit by the old base-burner and meditate and pray as I watched the red charcoal through the isinglass. It was a long and difficult struggle. It lasted many weeks. There was the matter of Alice not being a Baptist. She was a Methodist, though she went with me to church. There was the fact that I had never completed my college education. There was my complete ignorance of the demanding service in a new field. Too, I had never seen the Beaumont church, and had only once met their new pastor.

I guess the best way to say it is I was completely at the end of my rope. I felt helpless. Should I venture or not? I was conscious of "the still small voice" all through this agonizing decision. At last I found relief. I remembered Gideon had his fleece. I, too, would have my fleece. I prayed, "God, if you do not want me in your service, then keep the church from calling me. If the church calls I shall interpret it that you want me to go." I found peace of soul.

The church call came. I notified my father of my decision while he was vacationing in Colorado. Alice was baptized and joined the Baptist Church. I had never asked her to do so. It was a sure indication that she, too, wanted to dedicate her life to the cause of Christ, and walk by my side in all the work God gave us to do.

Soon Alice, Lois, our three-year-old daughter, and I were on our way in a new Graham-Paige car to a new work as Music and Educational Director of the First Baptist Church, Beaumont, Texas, a church I had never seen, which was six hundred miles away.

It pleased my father to see me make this decision since he did not preach as he felt the Lord directed him. He felt that somehow, through his son, he would make up to God for what he failed to do. Father's faith in me was one of those things which always encouraged me. I remember, just before I left for my new work, after I had sold my interest in the business to Father, he said, "Son, I have great faith in you that you will succeed, but wouldn't you like to retain your interest in the business, and if things do not turn out right, you can come back?" "No," I answered. "I am tearing down all bridges behind me, and sink or swim, live or die, I propose to work for the Lord all the rest of my life." I have always been glad I did it that way, for there were times afterward, when I felt myself insufficient for my task, I was tempted to return.

Before closing the story of my life at Wakita, I must relate two things that happened to me in connection with my Christian life, which had much to do with my Christian growth.

The first thing is tithing. I had never tithed, although it was my belief that a Christian should. After my marriage, my conscience bothered me all the more. But there were unexpected expenses all along the way. I once checked up and found I was deep in debt for me, but the sum was not much. I tried to make a bargain with the Lord, "Lord, get me out of debt and I will start to tithe." The result was I grew deeper in debt. What a tragedy to try to bargain with God! I needed to embrace the truth as taught in the Bible, and leave the results with the Lord. This I did. I began to tithe. I then had a clear conscience. What a joy tithing has brought in life. There has never been any guess work in regard to my gifts since that day. Tithing has been a practice of life.

The second thing is soul winning. Since my conversion, I had been too timid to try to win any person to Christ. Soul winning was too high and holy for me to attempt. An evangelist came to hold a revival in the Wakita church. After a week of fervent preaching with no visible results, he called a meeting at deacon Lemon's house. Had I known what the meeting was for, I might not have attended. The evangelist asked, "How many of you have spoken to anybody about being a Christian this week?" We dropped our heads in guilt. None of us had. If the evangelist had only stopped there! I would never have become a soul winner had he not gone on. He continued, "How many will promise God that before another day is gone, you will speak to someone about being a Christian?" I cannot forget the guilt I felt; I had known all along I should try to win people to Christ, but felt too weak a vessel to do it. I remembered that it was my older sister who helped me to Christ, and that I ought, in turn, to help someone else to find Him. I confess to my readers that I felt my legs were too weak for me to stand. On the other hand, I felt condemned before God if I did not stand. I stood, and I have always been grateful to the evangelist who forced me into soul winning, for ever since it has been the supreme joy of my life, and has become the main stream of my Christian service.

Beaumont Days

Everything was new to my family in Beaumont. We left the high, dry wheat lands of the prairie and arrived in the wet, low rice lands of the Gulf Coast. There were only a few miles of paved highways. One afternoon, the last of August 1919, we drove into Beaumont on Calder Avenue on oyster shelled roads to make our new home in among people we had never met, to begin a new work I knew nothing about, as a staff member of the First Baptist Church which I had never seen.

I had sought to find similar workers in other churches, but found none. There were a few assistants to the pastors and some song leaders. So it is said I went into this new field of music and education at its very beginning. It has often been said by Baptist leaders that I was the first in this field of Christian education. The name Minister of Education came later. I have been introduced as "the first Minister of Education as it is known today." This designation has also been applied to me in Baptist magazines and periodicals. In later years, when addressing pastors on the relationship of pastors and educational directors, I have said, "There have been pastors since Jesus came, but educational directors only for a short time. You keep working on us, and have patience, and give us time to catch up. Sometimes you do not know what to do with us, but it is a truth you cannot get along without us."

I have often said, about my first work at Beaumont, "When I arrived, the pastor did not know what I was to do; neither did the church; nor did I. We all started out even."

As churches grew, pastors needed help in their work. It was the usual custom for them to employ a member of the local church. A man would be found who could lead music, or a person who could secure pledges, or a man who was adept at organization. These workers would be paid a small sum for part or full time work. From this start came the field of religious education as it is known today. It is understandable, that in this process, there were many "square pegs in round holes," as we say.

Beaumont had been known as a lumber city. Many of its rich and leading citizens had gained their wealth in that industry. But by the time my family reached the city, it had become an oil metropolis. The old Spindle Top oil field had been discovered at the turn of the century. Too, Beaumont was a seaport. It was the seat of ship building during the First World War. Many ships were still anchored on the Neches River at the time of our arrival.

First Baptist Church was an elegant stone edifice located on Pearl Street. Across Forsythe Street, which ran along the south side of the church, was a park. The Young Men's Christian Association was next door, and the wharf was just beyond the park. The ferry crossed the Neches River less than two blocks away. I have many happy memories of my six years in Beaumont. It was my first church work, and as my "first love," the First Baptist Church there has ever been most dear to me.

Soon after my arrival, Southern Baptists launched their $75,000,000 Campaign. Our church entered into the project most heartedly. Those were challenging and exciting days. One Sunday throughout the South was designated "The Calling Out of the Called Day." Our pastor preached a sermon challenging young people to volunteer for special Christian service. At the close of the sermon, seventy-five young people had dedicated themselves to such service. Many who stood in that line became preachers, missionaries, and members of church staffs. Seldom, if ever, had any of us seen such a manifestation of the power of the Holy Spirit.

My Beaumont years were stirring days for me. The work was challenging, and the response of the people was so gratifying, that I poured my life into the work, day and night. I remember something that happened at our family dinner table which awakened me to my responsibility at home. As Alice, Babe and I dined, I said, "I am going to get to stay at home this evening." Presently, my daughter lifted her head, looked at her mother, and said, "Mama, is Papa the only company we are going to have tonight?" I never had anything to cut me more deeply. It was then and there I vowed not to let my church usurp the time I should devote to my family. Writing this life's story, fifty years after that event, I thank God that my daughter reminded me of my obligation to home. I needed to see to it that I should not give other parents' children the time I should devote to my own. Perhaps that is the reason, in retirement, I never go anywhere to any engagement without taking Mrs. Mead with me. That arrangement makes my retirement years more pleasant.

I took our church young people for a week every summer to the Palacios-by-the-Sea Encampment. I also led them to participate in associational and denominational affairs.

One thing which brought particular joy to me in Beaumont was that I taught a class of young men. This class grew to over 250 in enrollment, and we had as high as 150 in attendance in class on special occasions. What a joy was mine in winning many young men to Christ and helping them find their places in church work. Once they gave me a car. We called it the Agogabus for our class was named Agoga.

These were the days following the First World War, when there were very large classes in Sunday School. There were many classes with hundreds enrolled, and I knew of classes which numbered into the thousands. We had no Sunday School conventions in those days, but we had annual meetings for Organized Bible Class workers. We met 5,000 strong in Birmingham, Dallas, Shreveport, Hot Springs and other cities all over the South. I addressed the convention at one session in Hot Springs, Arkansas. Those were stirring and exciting days. Though I was inadequate, I threw myself into my work with abandon. I had help along the way, which will be revealed in the following paragraphs.

I wrote my dear maternal grandfather saying, "Grandfather, I wish I knew the Lord as well as you do so I could do a better job serving Him." He wrote back, giving encouragement, and added, "Earl, you can only know Jesus well by walking with Him. When you have walked with Him for fifty years as I have, you will know Him better." Now that I have walked with Jesus for over sixty years, I can understand what Grandfather said.

There was a dear saint of God in the church we called Mother Coleman. She was Dr. E. Y. Mullins' aunt. She took me under her wing and encouraged me and prayed for me. She called me "little pastor" though I was not a pastor then, or ever have been. One day I returned to my office and found Mother Coleman there by herself waiting for me. I said, "Mother Coleman, I am so sorry I left you here alone." Never can I forget that heavenly face, lit up with a sweet smile, as she said, "Why, little pastor, I am not alone. Jesus and I have been having the best time together." When

Mother Coleman left, I closed the door, got on my knees, and prayed ever so earnestly, "O God, help me to become conscious of the presence of Jesus in my daily life as Mother Coleman."

A member of that church was George Carroll, now retired. He had once been a rich man, but had lost his money because he trusted an unfaithful friend. He walked everywhere he went, and always carried an umbrella. Everybody loved and respected Brother Carroll. He often said to me, "The only money I ever saved was what I gave away." He was most generous with his gifts to Christian causes. He was known among Baptists all over Texas. A relative of mine by marriage, who was a girl at the time, and belonged to the Giddings Baptist Church, tells of this incident: In a prayer service, the pastor told about Brother Carroll's loss, and asked someone to pray for him. In the prayer, the man said, "Dear God, bless Brother Carroll and restore unto him the money he lost." A voice was heard above the prayer, "Yes, double it, Lord, double it."

My constant helper and inspiration in my work was my devoted wife. Not only was she devoted to her home, she was devoted to her church. She worked with the organizations of the church, and was Superintendent of the Intermediate Department in Sunday School. She continued to make this age group her charge as long as she lived. No one had a happier home base than I. Both wife and daughter stood by my side to encourage and abet me in the work the Lord had given me to do. God blessed our home and made it the spring-board for all our labors.

I served with three pastors at Beaumont. Dr. A. E. Booth, with whom I began, was a good preacher and a good organizer of men. He taught a class of 500 men in our Sunday School.

Following Dr. Booth's resignation, the church called Rev. B. W. Vining, who was one of the Texas Baptist leaders. Though he was pastor for over a year, he never preached a sermon. He became ill. The church gave half his salary till his death, with other funds coming in from other sources.

In the meantime the church had begun a new building in a different location in the city. This new edifice was almost completed when the church called Dr. J. W. Pace as pastor. I did not find it hard to adjust to these different personalities, and continued the best I could, to play "second fiddle" to my pastors. Each pastor made contributions to my life for which I have been eternally grateful.

The State Baptist leaders were kind to me and received me with open arms. Wm. P. Phillips was leader of the Texas Sunday School Department.

The inimitable T. C. Gardner led the Training Union Department. It was known then as the B. Y. P. U. There began to be groups for all ages, which changed the name to Baptist Training Union; however, before a family name was chosen by the Sunday School Department at Nashville, Texas had its own name; namely, The Baptist Training Service. Both these leaders used me on convention and conference programs.

In 1924 Dr. Arthur Flake of the Baptist Sunday School Board led in the first Sunday School Clinic. It was held in the Third Baptist Church, Owensburg, Kentucky. Dr. W. C. Boone was the pastor. We studied under Dr. Flake and his staff each morning, took a religious census and visited every afternoon, and joined the local church workers in study each evening. This clinic lasted three weeks and was a busy and profitable experience.

The First Baptist Church of San Antonio sought my services. Dr. I. E. Gates was the pastor. In spite of their call, I stayed with the Beaumont Church.

In the summer of 1925, I went to teach at the Arkansas Baptist Assembly at Siloam Springs. At the request of Dr. M. E. Dodd, I stopped in Shreveport to meet with a committee to consider the work of Educational Director of the First Baptist Church there. The church called me. During my stay at Siloam Springs, I prayed over my decision, and when I returned to Beaumont, I resigned and accepted the call of the Shreveport church. Thus I closed my six years of the most enjoyable work of my life at Beaumont, and left for my new assignment with the well wishes and prayers of the people.

I feel constrained to add a last word about my experiences at Beaumont. One experience had to do with whether I would continue my Christian work. My first pastor had resigned, but not of his own choosing. He was asked to resign because of behavior unbecoming a Christian leader. I had great faith in him, and could not believe in his moral laxity; however, it was found to be true. I had his flag at the top of the mast, but had to lower it. How crushing was the blow when I found my idol had crumbled. For days I was crushed, helpless, disillusioned. A vine falls to earth bleeding at every pore when its prop is gone. I do not know how things might have turned out for me, but for the fact, in my struggle, I vined myself around Jesus, in whom there is no imperfection. He became my sure prop. It was then, and only then, I regained faith and courage. I have never been disappointed in Jesus. He has never let me fall.

Shreveport's Wonderful Year

When I went with my family to Shreveport, Louisiana, in the fall of 1925, I knew I was to serve one of Southern Baptist's very influential and best known churches. It had one of the denomination's renowned pulpiteers, Dr. M. E. Dodd. He had been pastor of the First Baptist Church for over a quarter of a century.

Ministers of Education of this church in the past had short tenures of service. My friends, almost without exception, advised me not to go. But, after long agony and earnest prayer, I felt that God was leading me there, so I went.

What a wonderful year it was to be! I often refer to it by saying, "God's winds got in our sails." He moved us over a great and glorious sea. As I review my life, I can say I never had a happier year than in Shreveport.

Dr. Dodd was an indefatigable worker, and set the pace for me. He was also an able leader and revered pastor. He took me to his heart. Our partnership was made perfect through mutual respect and love for each other.

The educational organizations grew apace. In fact there were larger attendances in Sunday School and Training Union than ever before or since. A later educational director wrote:

"Dear Friend: What ever happened during your year at Shreveport? I have checked attendances, and find them to be higher in those days than at any time in the history of the church."

I told him, in my reply, that I could not account for it aside from the leadership and power of God. I added, as I have said before, "The winds of God got in our sails."

What a challenge the year was to me. As the pastor led, and God blessed, I followed. I was sailing on an expectant and expanding sea. Like the Apostle, on his last fishing trip, when he saw Jesus on the shore, "cast himself into the sea." So did I. And it was an experience of joy.

Soon after I arrived in Shreveport, a campaign was launched to build a girl's college to be located in the city. It was Dr. Dodd's dream to build a school for girls which would not only turn out graduates, but choice Southern belles as well. The First Baptist Church led in the campaign, with the Baptists of Louisiana to help. We gathered pledges, and the college became a reality. Later the school failed to get the support of the whole state, and the load was too much for First Church to carry by itself. This resulted in the closing of the college a few years after it opened. The school's closing was perhaps the greatest disappointment Dr. Dodd ever suffered.

To give some idea of the ties that bound the church and me together in love, I relate the following stories:

Once upon a return to Shreveport, a dinner was set in my honor by a dozen or more friends. Following the good and sweet fellowship, each person around the table arose to make love to me. Each added, "Mr. Mead, you put me to my first Christian work in the church." The surprise of my heart was only surpassed by my joy.

After I had been away from Shreveport for over thirty years, I returned with John Shanks and Mrs. Mead to meet a small group of old friends. They had asked us to check in at the Washington Youree Hotel. When we arrived and entered the lobby of the hotel, I read on a big chart, "The J. Earl Mead banquet is held in the Crystal Ballroom." Entering our room I found it to be the bridal suite and filled with flowers. Surprised and in wonderment, we dressed and proceeded to the banquet hall. There to my delight and surprise were gathered over two hundred of my old church associates and fellow workers. The whole affair was arranged, and probably mostly financed, by my good friend Baylor Culpepper. I had enlisted him and his late wife in leading Intermediates in Training Union long ago. After the banquet I led a cottage prayer meeting in the Culpepper's home, which was attended by over one hundred people.

Across the years, I have returned to Shreveport to teach and speak in churches, and in huge area-wide study courses. On each return I have fellowship with old First Church friends with whom I had worked in my Shreveport days.

After fifty years I returned to preach from that famous pulpit at the invitation of the pastor James Middleton. Again I was blessed by old friends.

I learned long ago that Christian friends are prized possessions. When one devotes a life time to serving churches, it does not mean he retires with big bags of money. The opposite is true. His riches are in his friends. I have come to prize these friends, and have become rich in friendships.

I now come to a time which tried my soul. Before leaving Beaumont for Shreveport, Dr. Wallace Bassett, pastor of Cliff Temple Baptist Church, Dallas, had come to be the preacher for the Southeast Baptist Association Encampment held in Magnolia Park. I was President of that encampment. It was "love at first sight" between us. Before the encampment was over, Dr. Bassett said to me, "Earl, if Old Hop ever leaves me I am coming for you." Old Hop was G. S. Hopkins, who at the time was Minister of Education at Cliff Temple.

I began my work in Shreveport on September 1, 1925. By the end of the year, Hopkins had resigned at Cliff Temple to become the Sunday School Secretary of Texas Baptists. Dr. Bassett called to remind me of what he said in Beaumont, and asked me to come to succeed Mr. Hopkins. Of course, I had only begun my Shreveport work and felt I must decline the invitation.

Time moved along until February 1926. I attended the Organized Bible Class Convention at Birmingham, Alabama. Dr. Bassett and one of his members were there. They pressed me the second time to come to Cliff Temple. Dr. Bassett said, "As long as we feel as we do about it, we will never call anybody else." I replied, "As long as I feel as I do about it, I will never come." Thus we parted.

I kept hearing that Cliff Temple was still without an Educational Director. During my summer's vacation, my family stopped in Dallas to visit Dr. Fred Eastham and his wife Wanda. Dr. Eastham had graduated from Beaumont High School the year I had arrived. We had become fast friends. In fact, during a time of distress and trouble at Beaumont, Fred came down to see me and was alarmed at how fatigued I was. He persuaded the deacons to give me a few days' release from my work. Then he and Wanda took me to a retreat in the Big Thicket above Silsbee, and there we spent several days together.

During my Beaumont days, I had gone duck hunting with Fred in the coastal swamps. How cold was that day! When ducks were flying in, Fred would say, "Get down." I would squat in that cold water only to see the ducks disappear overhead too high to shoot, or veer to the side. When I got home that night, with no ducks, and was hungry and tired I said to Alice, "If I ever go hunting for ducks in the swamps again, I want you to hit me over the head with a baseball bat." That one experience was never repeated.

To resume my story of our stop in Dallas: I asked Fred to take me by Cliff Temple Baptist Church, so I could have a look at it. We then returned to Shreveport to resume my work. I never knew until much later that Fred had called Dr. Bassett to tell him I had been by to see the church.

I devoted myself to getting a good start in the fall work. One morning, after arising, and before going to the office, Dr. Bassett called to say he was in Shreveport. His church had sent him to try again to persuade me to come to Dallas. He felt I should meet his committee as a matter of courtesy. This I thought I should do for Dr. Bassett's sake. I reported my intended trip to Dr. Dodd before going. I met the Dallas committee and returned without changing my mind.

Again Dr. Bassett called to say it had been almost a year since the church had had an Education Director. "If you will not come, we are forced to call somebody else." By this time I was greatly distressed. How could God impress that church that they should call me, and impress me that I should remain? That was a riddle. One of us had to be wrong.

Dr. Bassett set a dead line, and said, "If you change your mind, call." I let the dead line pass, and in a day or so became so distraught that I called Dr. Bassett to ask about details to try to get more light on the subject. Dr. Bassett informed me, that since I had not called, they had offered the place to Dr. George Mason. Instantly and eagerly, I took that as my Gideon's fleece. I said, "If George Mason accepts, we will take it to mean that you were wrong and I was right. But if he does not accept, I will come." I was relieved to know that it was now entirely in the hands of God.

George Mason turned the church down. The next morning Dr. Bassett was in Shreveport and I began to plan my departure for Dallas.

Dr. Dodd was in Columbus, Ohio. I felt I should let him know of my decision. I consulted a faithful deacon. He advised me to wait until the pastor returned. But since my acceptance of the position would soon be printed in the Dallas newspapers, I felt I had to contact Dr. Dodd. I wanted to inform him, but I promised to await my formal resignation until his return.

I can never forget Dr. Dodd's telegram in reply. Now, fifty years later, I can almost quote Dr. Dodd's telegram verbatim. It read, "I am surprised, disappointed, hurt. You promised me and told the people Cliff Temple was a closed incident. Your going practically means my end at Shreveport. I am wiring Dr. Bassett I do not appreciate his persistence. Do nothing further until I return."

After Dr. Dodd returned, I tried to see him before Sunday, but to no avail. On Sunday, he announced from the pulpit my intention, and added, "As far as I am concerned, he goes over my protest." Applause followed the announcement. I had never heard applause in that sanctuary before. There I sat with my family, knowing I had to go, for I had found God's will. The following Sunday the young people asked me to join them at a sunrise prayer meeting. They wanted me to stay, but this, I knew I could never do.

I have never known fully why I spent only one year at Shreveport and almost thirty-seven years at Cliff Temple in Dallas. Maybe the one thing which was so appealing to me was the fact that at that time Cliff Temple was building three four-story buildings for educational expansion. The church at Shreveport made no effort to build for educational work in spite of the fact we had classes in the Y. M. C. A., the lodge building and the *Shreveport Times* building. Cliff Temple was a pulpit and teaching church while the Shreveport church was mostly a preaching church.

Pursuing the Work
At Cliff Temple

When I arrived in Dallas to take up my work as Minister of Education at Cliff Temple, I was aware that I had come to a thriving metropolis to serve in a fast growing church, with a pastor who put emphasis on the Sunday School. Dr. Wallace Bassett was big in any way one measured him. He was big of body, big of brain, big of heart, and big of soul. There was no littleness in him. He was the guide and inspiration of his church staff as well as the church membership. He was sought far and wide over the Southern Baptist Convention for revivals, preacher conferences, and conventions. He was an inspiring leader, and always happy to share the love of the people with his staff. He was as much my ideal after serving with him for over thirty-six years as the day he became my pastor. No word of criticism concerning him ever escaped my lips about my pastor, nor had he ever given me any cause for such. He had been with Cliff Temple eight years before I arrived in 1926, and stayed four years after my retirement in 1962, which gave him forty-eight years as Cliff Temple's pastor.

As I stated above, Dr. Bassett put emphasis on the teaching ministry of the church. Soon after I came to be with him, he said, "Earl, I had one goal when I came to Cliff Temple, and that was to build a big Sunday School, which I knew, in turn, would build a great church." That dream of his came true, for Cliff Temple became one of the very large churches of the Southern Baptist Convention.

He continued to talk about those early days. "I sent for Old Hop (meaning G. S. Hopkins, my predecessor), and when he came I thought we were sunk, for he began to spend much time teaching little books." Then, he concluded, "I found he hit upon the thing which brought about the growth and effectiveness of our Sunday School."

Later I told Dr. Hopkins, who at the time was State Sunday School Secretary for Texas Baptists, what Dr. Bassett had said. He smiled, and replied, "You know I had worked at the post office in Amarillo and knew little about Sunday School work, so about all I knew to do was to teach Sunday School training course books."

By the time Dr. Hopkins resigned, Cliff Temple was at the top, or near the top of the list of earned awards by Sunday School workers. The church had graduation day every fall at which time it recognized these trained workers and issued their certificates after a graduation oration by some noted person. These certificates were displayed on every wall of the sanctuary's foyer.

So ingrained was necessary training in the minds of the workers that, when I came, I still emphasized training. When I finished teaching a book, the teachers would ask, "When are you going to teach another book?" I would smilingly reply, "Just as soon as I catch my breath."

I kept training at the heart of my work, and had a well planned schedule of teaching books throughout the year, many of which I taught myself. Every Thursday was given to teaching. I began by teaching morning classes. Then I tried evening classes. But soon I taught both Thursday morning and evening, pupils to take their choice. This meant five hours of teaching every Thursday for me. I used to say, "I practice on the morning class and teach the evening class."

We led Cliff Temple to participate in training schools with other churches in the Dallas Baptist Association. For several years, Dr. Hopkins, our State Sunday School Secretary, planned such schools in February in the large cities of Texas. I remember one February I was the speaker at a banquet of Dallas Sunday School workers at Fair Park at which over fifteen hundred people were in attendance. These great schools meant much to the growth and spirit of all our Sunday Schools. Training may not attract workers in great numbers, but one can train many people in classes of ten and twenty over thirty-six years.

Enlisting workers and people must be emphasized before they are trained. There was always the matter of visiting and finding people. We sought newcomers to Dallas and old residents as well. Plans had to be inaugurated and perfected which would send workers out into the community. All through the years of my ministry at Cliff Temple, we observed and maintained days of visitation. Two hundred or more workers participated in these visitation activities. This resulted in a group unity, a deepening commitment, and a warm Christian spirit. It also resulted in an ever-growing Sunday School and church.

The Sunday School had gained such prominence over the Southern Baptist Convention that a constant stream of workers from other churches came to see it and study the plans which brought it about. Twenty-five hundred in Sunday School was low for the school, and often there were more than three thousand present.

Before leaving the matter of visitation, I must speak a personal word. Visitation was not only for our workers, it was for me, also. How I enjoyed spending a day knocking at doors, meeting new people, and giving them a cordial invitation to come to Cliff Temple. Visitation was among my most pleasurable experiences. I felt somehow I was more like the Master on those days. The Bible states, "He went about doing good." He went into the synagogue, as his custom was, but by far most of his time was spent out among the people. At the end of visitation days, I always went home with a happy heart by nightfall.

But of all the things I did, I liked soul winning best. No greater joy ever came to my heart than the joy of soul winning. Constantly, I gave myself to seeking the lost for the Savior. One day one of our faithful members said to me, "Will you please go to see my husband? He is not a Christian and has no use for the church; in fact, he may insult you and tell you to leave, but will you please go to see him?" Of course, I promised. Soon I was on my way to see the unsaved man. I had never met him. "What will I find?" I asked myself. I knocked at the door, and I heard the tump of his cane, for he was a crippled man. He greeted me. I told him who I was. He knew me through his wife's reports. His little grandson was presented. Being a grandfather myself, I knew I had no chance of getting the man's full attention. In a moment a neighborhood boy came out and shouted for his little playmate. Grandfather put the boy's coat on, and soon he was gone. How wonderfully God works on such occasions. Now my thought was, "How shall I begin?" God worked that out, too. The unsaved man limped to the fireplace and lifted a Bible from the mantel, and said, "Mr. Mead, my wife's Sunday School Class gave me this Bible." In a moment I had the Bible in my hand telling the man how to be saved. The man trusted Christ and joined the church. Much later I preached this man's funeral. How glad I was that the first time I had seen him I won him to Christ.

Take the case of the teen-aged country girl, who moved to our city. She came to our church for the first time. Just before the evening preaching service, some of our young people came and said, "Mr. Mead, there is a new girl back here who wants somebody to tell her how to become a Christian." Immediately, I walked to the girl's pew, shook hands with her, introduced myself, and said, "Someone told me that you wanted somebody to tell you how to become a Christian." She answered, "Yes, I do." Then we set a date, and on that evening she accepted Christ as her personal Savior.

These are only two of many instances of a multitude of occasions when I was on the road with my Lord in soul winning.

Dr. Bassett, pastor, led over seventy revivals in his own church. I mean by that, that he did the preaching. In such meetings, it always fell my lot twice a year to lead the soul winners. We would prepare for these revivals by calling our teachers and workers to join a soul winning band. We would meet for preparation, assignments, and prayer. At such times I always had every teacher to write down the names of the lost in their classes. In adult classes where most were Christians, I would ask for the names of members of the families who were unsaved. During the revival week we would meet for prayer and go on errands of soul winning. If our workers responded to the call for prayer and soul winning, revival always resulted. I could always tell by the response of our workers, if a real revival was to be experienced.

To show how much a revival depends on the response of Christians themselves I relate the following experiences:

One revival week Dr. Bassett said, "Earl, this week I will only preach on Sundays and Wednesday night. We will use the other days of the week for visiting and soul winning." The plan the pastor laid out was for our soul winners to bring those they had won to the Lord as guests to the Wednesday night dinner. There at the table, each of us sat by the person, or persons, who would join the church that night. As we left the dining room to meet in the sanctuary for the preaching service, Dr. Bassett said to me, "I am not going to preach a long sermon tonight." I replied, "You do not have to preach at all for we will have twenty-six additions to the church." I was wrong. Only twenty-five joined. One backed out. Mrs. Mead and I had four couples as our guests that night.

Bear with me for another revival experience. The last revival in which I participated before my retirement in the spring of 1962, we had ninety-nine additions to the church by baptism. Dr. Wade Freeman was the preacher. It was a people's revival. Although there was no shouting, the people were happy at heart because they were soul winners themselves, and brought their friends and neighbors to Christ. Dr. Bassett's comment on the baptizing was, "I made a mistake tonight. I should have baptized that three hundred pound man first instead of ninety-ninth, for I was plumb tuckered out when I got to him."

To show the soul winners' part in revival, I recall the revival Dr. Dodd held in the Shreveport church while I was there. He called us in for counsel and said, "This will be an eight-day revival. I will preach day and night, but with no invitation to sinners and the unchurched except on the last Sunday. But this I intend to do: When I finish my sermon each time I preach, I am going to ask those who have won a soul to Christ today, or got someone to promise to join the church next Sunday, to come forward and join the line before me." I thought that I had never heard of a revival like that in my life, and wondered about it. But that wise pastor knew wherein the failure or success of revival lay. As a soul winner, and a member of that church and staff, I stood in that line every night. When the last Sunday came, the pastor gave the invitation for salvation and church membership and one hundred eleven people came forward.

In speaking about growth in our numbers in Sunday School, I should have mentioned the growth in our Baptist Training Union also. We had many unions of members from children through the adults. I might say the young people swarmed around Cliff Temple. Our leaders were trained and dedicated. Our church sent them to the Training Union State Conventions annually. We led the state in attendance at these Sunday evening meetings and insofar as I know the south. Our average attendance was around eight hundred, and our biggest attendance ran over two thousand. Those were exciting and thrilling times.

Relationships with Church Staffs
And Church Leaders

One of my chief concerns and joys in church work all along the way has been the fellowship and labor with members of the church staff. All of us had one thing in common: namely, we had wholly committed ourselves to serving the Lord. We had gone into the schoolroom of life with our compass, pencil and paper, and, as it were, drew a circle and in the center put a cross standing for Christ, and in that circumference put a dot representing ourselves somewhere serving our Lord. Christ was first, the church second, the pastor third, and the church members fourth. We were last. We were just servants of the Lord, rejoicing in the progress of the church, thankful to God that He let us have a part in it.

Church staffs, when I went into church work in 1919, were small in all instances. But they grew apace across the years until now big churches have so many staff members that I sometimes say in jest, "They remind me of the Pentagon Building." In past days, most church work was done by the members themselves, but since the churches have the money with which to do it, when the pastor suggests something else be done, church leaders tell the pastor to find someone for the job, and the church will pay the salary. I do not know if that is the best way for work to progress, but it is common practice anyway.

We always had the weekly conferences with staff members under the direction of the pastor, unless he delegated that responsibility to another member of the staff. Dr. Bassett, with whom I worked so long, never liked such conferences, which called for so many details, so it fell my lot to lead these Monday morning conferences for over thirty-six years.

This conference would include the typists and secretaries as well as those leading in music, Christian education, youth work. Here we would review what had transpired the week before, and talk about the pastor's plans for the work immediately ahead. It was here we "repaired our fences." This informed every one present of what the church was about in its programming, and the part of each staff member in bringing it to pass. It brought about a correlation of every segment of our church work, and made every worker feel he or she had a vital part in it. It tied us together as a team in fellowship and action.

It was our practice to have staff members and their spouses in our home during the year. Mrs. Mead was the center of this activity, bless her. Always she shared my responsibilities, and the home was ever open to receive our visitors. There was the Mexican dinner prepared and served by Mrs. Mead (Lois). At Christmas time we had the staff for a big dinner. It was a happy family that gathered around our table. In the summer time, this group met on our back lawn for a hamburger supper. All this brought our staff members together in sweet fellowship, genuine comradeship, and perfect partnership and understanding. I had a deep love for every staff member in the three churches I served, and an abiding appreciation for them and their work. To this good day they pass before my mind in review and I love them all. I owe them a deep debt of gratitude for their contributions to my life. They greatly blessed me and aided me in my work. They are too many to name.

I also magnified my close contact with the church leaders. At a monthly luncheon meeting, at which all our departments were represented, we maintained an almost perfect attendance. After dining, we handed out typewritten sheets showing some of our accomplishments, thanking them for bringing such things to pass. Then we spread before them the work which was before us. It was big enough to be a challenge to each and all. Before leaving the meeting, our pastor would pray for the work ahead, asking for God's blessings upon our conjoined efforts.

I always referred to this meeting as "our power house." It brought diligent work, sweet fellowship, and complete cooperation to the whole group. Full cooperation was always needed in a big church. At Cliff Temple there were so many buildings, so many floors, so many partitions which divided us, we had to magnify the work as a whole so that every teacher, every leader, every deacon might be lead to keep step as our vast army marched forward. I remember a meeting once in which I asked the pastor to put the "capsheaf" on at the close. "Now," he said, "every worker must pitch to the center. If you do not you cannot - -" and here he was stuck for a word. He paused and he stammered and said, "If you don't pitch to the center, you can't domino." Well, he got the right word, for without full cooperation, the program cannot be accomplished. "The center" in a church is where the man of God stands at the pulpit. He thinks more, dreams more, and plans more for the church than all the rest of us put together.

Another thing I did to show my personal interest in every leader was to send them a personal greeting on their birthdays. I kept a book in which were listed the names of my teachers and leaders with the day and month of their births. Every Monday morning I would write personal greetings to those whose birthdays fell on that week.

Before my annual vacations, which were usually in the Rocky Mountains, I would have my secretary address envelopes to all these workers numbering over two hundred. Then while on vacation, I would write each a personal letter. These things I did to make a bond of love and fellowship between us.

In the late summer, before our big fall program was to be launched, Mrs. Mead and I would invite our Sunday School teachers and officers to our house. We invited them in departmental groups beginning with the workers with children and on up through the adults. We had them on Tuesdays and Thursdays for six weeks. Each group met on the lawn in the early evenings. The meetings were devoted to prayer, testimony, and a personal word of appreciation by me. Then, after refreshments of fruit juices and homemade cookies, the meetings were adjourned.

If teachers were tired and weary, discouraged, or thinking about resigning, this meeting often resulted in their being buoyed up, and they went on to face coming responsibilities with renewed zest. I remember on one occasion we had hosted the pre-school teachers and officers. To open the meeting I arose to thank these faithful workers for their faithfulness. Then I added, "I put this chair out tonight for the Lord. I want all of us to feel that He is as much present as all of us." After prayer there was testimony. Mrs. Ralph Whipple, a faithful superintendent arose. I could see a trace of tears in her eyes as she said, "I came here tonight to resign, but since Mr. Mead has made us conscious of God's presence by putting out a chair for Him, if God will forgive me and Mr. Mead will let me, I will go on." This dear lady, who had served so long, got her second wind, so to speak, and continued to work until by reason of passing time had to quit.

I have always said, "Every teacher wants to resign now and then." I tried to anticipate these times and give words of encouragement in order to prevent it. I have heard teachers say, "I came to Mr. Mead intending to resign and turn in my books, only to be so encouraged that I did not resign, and left with my books under my arm." There was one thing said about me which I considered a compliment. "I just cannot resign to Mr. Mead," they would say. I guess it was because I had so much faith in them that they did not want to disappoint me.

There was inaugurated an annual Educational Rally. This was set for late August or early September before our fall program was launched. In fact, the fall program was launched at that meeting. It was a sort of roll call meeting though no personal roll call was observed. All church members who had an elected or appointed office were expected to attend. The deacons, choir members, Woman's Missionary Auxiliaries, Sunday School forces, and Training Union leaders were all present. We would have each group stand for recognition. Then their respective leaders would pledge them to renewed dedication and work. Ours was a big church, thus we would have over eight hundred people present. Even if no program had been planned at all, the excitement and encouragement engendered by this vast crowd worked wonders in the hearts of our leaders. I would bring my annual challenge to the group. Then the meeting was closed by a prayer of dedication. This would sweep us into a presentation of challenging goals. The whole organization was a moving, throbbing, spirit-filled aggregation ready for the labors ahead. The workers were excited, expectant, as they anticipated sailing on this expansive Sea of God. The spiritual winds of God filled our sails and we addressed ourselves to the work He had given us to do in the days ahead. We felt God's presence and guidance, and through the leadership of our pastor and his inspiration, we kept stretched out in the work of soul winning, teaching, stewardship and missions.

To encourage workers to stay in service for a long period of time, I put photographs of all those who had served in the same place at Cliff Temple for twenty years in our weekly paper. I displayed these photos in the foyers and halls of our buildings. I was surprised to see such a large number of them. Both Dr. Bassett and I were in that group, as well as others on the church staff. I feel that this obtained results in lengthening the service of those in the work.

Another practice which had a good and lasting effect on our workers and on my relationship with them, was that the church encouraged the superintendents of Sunday School and the leaders in Training Union to attend the annual State conventions. Not only did the church encourage such attendance, it helped defray their expenses incurred. It was a way the church had of showing appreciation for its leaders. Such meetings widened the horizons of our leaders, kept them informed of changes and newest methods, and greatly added to the moving spirit of our forces.

Staying close to the staff and church leaders was my earnest desire, and I have recorded here some of the things I did to bring this close association about. Walking with such dedicated and able workers sweetened my journey and brought joy to my heart all along the way.

Sorrows and Trials on the Way

The years of service lengthened at Cliff Temple. How comfortable was my nest! How challenging the days! How manifest was God's presence and guidance! I felt like the Apostle John; namely, that I was the disciple Jesus loved, so bountiful were his blessings to me. My family, my church, my work were great joys to me. My happiness knew no bounds as one blessed year succeeded another.

Then in 1948, after twenty-two years at Cliff Temple, came a deep sorrow and an agonizing trial. I had gone to Oklahoma on an engagement, and turned aside to visit my aging father on the way home. I boarded a train at Enid, Oklahoma, and on the way to Dallas the train stalled on the track, and there we stayed for ten hours with no heat. It was wintertime, and the weather was frigid. We arrived in Dallas many hours late, and I had a sore throat. Though not a preacher, I was to begin a revival at Westmount, a mission of Cliff Temple. In spite of the fact I had a genuine case of laryngitis when the meeting began, I attempted it, though speaking in a hoarse voice. God blessed us, and there were thirty-eight additions to the church.

After the meeting, I had grave trouble with my voice. I remember, when Vacation Bible School time came, I led the songs and scriptures by moving my lips only. The pastor and deacons, seeing my condition, ordered me off for a rest. "Take all the time you need to regain your voice," the spokesman said. I had done the rounds of Arkansas with leaders some time before, and one day's meeting had been at Harrison, on the fringe of the tourist resorts in the Ozarks. I chose this place for our retreat. Alice, who was never physically strong, was suffering from asthma. We both needed rest. We found a snug nest in a motel with log cottages, a lovely place for such a withdrawal from work. I remember well those days when Alice labored to breathe, and when I could not utter a word. I would arise at dawn and go for a walk down the country lanes to study birds and wild flowers. Every farmer had hounds which barked at me as I passed. Upon returning to the log cabin, I would write a note to ask Alice how she felt. "Not well," she answered. A letter came from the deacons, urging us to take all the time we needed to get well.

After two weeks we were unimproved, so we decided home was the place for us. So we drove home. Knowing, by now, I needed medical attention with my voice trouble, I immediately went to see a doctor. As he examined me he said, "Say ah." I tried but failed. Then the doctor announced, "Your speaking days are over." He diagnosed my trouble as myasthenia larynges, which I learned was trouble with the muscles of the larynx. For a moment, my world crashed about me. What could I do? I had to have the use of my voice to carry on my work.

The announcement came on a week-end. Sunday was the Fourth of July. Monday was a holiday. On Tuesday, I went to my office to meet the staff in conference as our custom was. I said to Alice, as I left home, "I shall tell the staff I will never speak again." I am sure Alice felt the blow as keenly as I. Her last words to me were, "Promise me you will come home by noon." I promised. When the staff met, I wrote a note and passed it. The note read, "The doctor says I will never speak again." I cannot describe the pathos of that hour; not can I ever forget the silent tears which began to course down the cheeks of those present – tears of love and sympathy.

I found that my long-time and cherished friend J. B. Christian, our music director and part-time worker at a local funeral home, was to drive an ambulance to a local hospital to take a mother and newborn son home. Knowing the mother, I asked to go along. When I returned to the office, I called home but got no answer. I called Babe, my daughter, to ask if she knew where her mother was and found Alice had gone to a neighbor's to return something she had borrowed. I rang the neighbor. "Yes, Alice is here and has suddenly become very ill," the neighbor said. I rushed to Alice's side and found our family physician already there. Alice had suffered a massive brain stroke. She never recognized me in the throes of this sudden stroke.

By mid-afternoon of July 6, 1948, Alice was gone. On Thursday, July 8, the funeral service was held in Cliff Temple's sanctuary. Dr. Bassett was at home recovering from an operation so Dr. Fred Eastham, pastor of the First Baptist Church, Springfield, Missouri, preached Alice's funeral. J. B. Christian sang, with his son joining him in a duet. I had known Brother Fred in 1919, when he had just graduated from high school. His family and mine had been fast friends almost thirty years. His tribute to Alice was in three parts: contentment with her lot, her capabilities, and her deep spirituality. Alice's body was laid to rest in Laurel Land cemetery, south of Oak Cliff. She had been my right hand, my counselor, my constant inspiration, and my strength. Now I was bereft. Gentle Alice was by my side no more, and my voice was gone.

As soon as it was known about Alice's sudden home-going our friends came, the chairman of deacons, Gus Berry, and our family physician, Dr. L. C. Sams among them. I sent these two men to see Dr. Bassett to inform him of Alice's death and to inform him of what the doctor said about my voice. I could not talk to them, so I sent them with a note. They soon returned with my pastor's sympathetic words. Then they added this from the pastor, "Tell Earl I had rather have him with no voice than any other educational director in the South." What a message from my great pastor. I had a growing awareness that without my voice I could not carry on in my work, but this message was one of the most precious experiences of my life, and was the word I needed for this crisis.

Soon it was time for our new fall's work and I without a word to promote it. I remember one Wednesday night at prayer meeting; Dr. Bassett asked me if I had a word about the coming program. I had a thousand words but unable to say even one. I arose, and with my hands motioned to describe the north wind which denoted the coming of fall, and took my seat. Those present knew what I meant, for every fall I would speak of the first north breeze which would cool the days for our work ahead. I would also talk about the inland plover flying over head in the darkness, calling to his mate as they flew southward. I would speak of the first skittering leaf on the pavement, and the first general rain which broke the drought and heat of summer, and the crickets that gathered under the arc lights. Often some would say to me at this time of year, "Mr. Mead, when are you going to start your plovers flying south?"

Having been around death constantly in my work, it was no strange word to me. I had wept with others on such occasions, and now they wept with me. Alice and I had talked about the possibility of such an event, and how the remaining partner should take it. I knew from whence my strength came, and so, in this extremity, I leaned heavily upon my Lord, and found Him sufficient. So, with my hand in His, I walked with Him through "the valley of the shadow," contained my tears and bore my sorrow and loss, as a Christian ought.

But what about my voice? I do not clearly remember if I whined or complained. If I did, I now ask God to forgive me. Did you ever go a whole year without speaking? I ran upon this phrase, "When you speak low, speak love." So I went around making love to everybody. When going to a meeting, as I got into the car, I would write, "I can't speak so give me some edifying conversation as we ride along."

I learned more about the Lord that year without a voice than in all other times put together. I leaned on God in my distress and depended upon Him for guidance. I used to jokingly say, "If only one would remain silent, he might hear some good conversation now and then."

I cannot over-state what the pastor, the staff and our leaders meant to me in those trying days. They were patient, kind and tolerant, and I leaned heavily upon their love and prayers.

For a whole year, when the workers' council met, I had to write my message and have it read by someone present. I wrote nine messages during the year. We dispensed with this meeting during the three summer months. The first one of my messages was on "Love's Renewal," which I here set down. It was printed on the first page of *The Baptist Standard* in September, 1948.

(*Baptist Standard* Editor's note: Mr. Mead, who lost both his beloved wife and his voice in a summer's time, distributed copies of this message, which he called "My Speech" at the monthly workers' meeting of his church on September 8.)

Love's Renewal

The day has arrived, the hour now strikes, and God begins to gently but surely draw the curtain which reveals the stage upon which we are to play our particular roles in the coming year. Are you ready?

Am I ready? Not if there is something wrong between me and God. Not if anything is wrong between me and anybody else in the whole wide world. Not if my work holds little attraction for me. Not if I have to be compelled from without instead of being impelled from within.

There is nothing we face between this milestone and our next that can deter or harm us – not even sorrow or death. There is nothing we face but victory if things are right in our hearts. The Lord is Master of all and over all. So we put our hands in His and join hands together then face the future with confidence as our hearts strike up God's song for the journey.

How I have yearned to make one speech as we begin our fall's work. I got the subject from *The Bishop's Mantle*.

Love's renewal was a message for me this summer up in God's hills. With the dawn each morning I was out with my binoculars tramping the trails, eyes and ears keenly alerted for God's sights and sounds. Like the morning dew which refreshed the earth, I prayed for the dew of Heaven to bring renewal to my spirit. The rising sun, the gentle wind, the blue sky, the rippling water, the birds' musical choruses, and all things spoke to me of Love's Renewal. It was love's renewal for Elijah after Carmel which sent him back to God's work. It was love's renewal for Jacob when he wrestled the angel at Jabbok. It was love's renewal for Peter when he had breakfast with the risen Lord. Then I remembered what the Lord said to the church at Ephesus, "I have somewhat against thee because thou hast left thy first love."

So while resting in the hills, Alice seeking relief from asthma, and I the return of my voice, I had earnestly prayed, "Give me love's renewal, O God; renewal and refreshment for the work Thou hast ordained me to do. Amen!" And now without voice to make my speech, and without gentle Alice's wise daily counsel, I know I shall find his burden easy, his yoke light, since he has given me a renewal of love for the journey. Have you experienced love's renewal for what lies ahead of you?

And thus ended what I had written on "Love's Renewal."

One day I walked into my office and looked out the window. I saw nothing, for my mind was occupied with thoughts about having no voice. I remember the exact day well. I prayed, "Dear God, I shall never complain again about having no voice. If you want to trust me with a voice, I shall use it for Thee all the days of my life." Was it from that day I began to regain my voice? I do not know; maybe so. I know this: My voice began to return, slowly but surely. I could only speak briefly and low at first, then the voice became stronger and stronger. My preacher friends and others would say, "I prayed for you. I knew you would speak again." My cure came from no doctor, but by the help and grace of God, and I thank Him for it. I do not abuse it for it is His, and I have dedicated it to His service for life. I have spoken more since that day than in all the days before. How precious it is to lift my voice in testimony of His love and care everywhere I go.

My Work
With the Baptist Denomination

I was always interested in Baptist work beyond the confines of my own local church. I never thought it right to be so consumed with labors in my own church that I could not join hands with my brothers in other churches. I often said to my fellow ministers of education, when inviting them to participate in our Religious Education and Music Association affairs, "If you are too busy to come, you are too busy."

During the years of my service I have had young pastors confide in me, "There are some things I don't like in the work of our denomination." They would continue their criticisms, and often add, "Sometimes I feel like going it alone." My word to them was, "Stay in, and try to correct the things you think are wrong."

Two young men came to see me with their grievances. One said, "We don't think the preacher's sermons are as they should be." I answered, "Since the good Lord called him to preach, I am going to leave it to Him to give the pastor his sermons." The other said, "We don't think some of our deacons are living right." It was then I replied, "Young men, did it ever occur to you that as long as the three of us belong to this church, it cannot be perfect?" That terminated the conversation. They arose to leave and said, "Good-bye, Mr. Mead." I said, "Goodbye, boys." They left thinking of their own imperfections and not those of other church members.

I liked walking along with the leaders in our State and Southwide. I was personally dedicated to cooperation with Baptists everywhere. I often spoke and led conferences in the churches in Dallas County, and always answered their calls for service. They showed their appreciation by choosing me to serve in the capacity of president, or chairman, or trustee.

In the late 1930s, I served as President of the Texas Training Union Convention. I was elected President of the Texas Sunday School Convention in 1941. I was President of the Religious Education and Music Conference of Dallas Baptist Association. I served as President of the Southwestern Baptist Religious Education Association in 1936.

I was elected Secretary of the Corporation for the Texas Baptist General Convention in 1946 to succeed Robert H. Coleman. This position I have held since then, to the time of this writing, 1978. This means I have also been a member of the Texas Baptist Executive Board all these years.

I served Southern Baptists as a member of the Sunday School Board of Trustees for two consecutive years and was chosen President of the Board for two consecutive years. Up to that time I was the only Minister of Education ever to serve as president of this group. I was happy that the group thus honored a member of my profession.

I was appointed by the Southern Baptist Convention as a member of a Correlation Committee. Our chairman was Dr. Gaines Dobbins, head of the Christian Education Department of the Southern Seminary. This committee was charged with the responsibility of recommending a church training study course. At that time Southern Baptists had several training courses for various departments of the church life. The committee's recommendations were accepted and this over-all training course helped to correlate the work of our churches, and magnified the church in the minds of the members.

I was invited to participate in State and Southwide meetings, conferences, and conventions. I taught and spoke in summer assemblies and camps. I helped in city-wide and associational-wide training schools in and out of Texas. Thus I came in contact with Baptist leaders all over the convention. Because of my length of service and its wide extent, I was fairly well known among my brethren. The friendship of these workers I value very highly, and they have added joy to my life.

It was probably because of participation in denominational work that I became recipient of honors from Baptist groups. In the spring of 1962, I resigned my position at Cliff Temple. The following day I had a letter from the President of Baylor University asking me to bring the baccalaureate address to Baylor graduates. For one day I had shed the burden of my work, only to pick it up again as I prepared my message. I spoke on the text, "Now the disciples had forgotten to take bread." (Mark 8:14). I urged the graduates not to forget to take bread to a hungering world. The next day, May 25, 1962, at the graduation exercises, Baylor conferred upon me the honorary degree of Doctor of Laws.

At Old Independence, where Texas Baptists began, I was honored to receive the award as Elder Statesman of Texas Baptists on Sunday, June 5, 1977. There were five things which made this a most significant event for me; namely, first, it was held in the old historic Baptist church where Burleson attended with Baylor students, and where Sam Houston was converted. A flag still marks the pew where Houston sat when he came to worship. Second, every member of my immediate family living in Texas was in attendance. Even my four-year-old great-grandson, Barton Thrasher, was there. Third, there was a good representation from Cliff Temple, where I had served so long. Fourth, the plaque was presented by Jay Skaggs, who had served with me on Cliff Temple's staff. Fifth, it was a signal honor to join other Baptist leaders, who had been chosen for this high honor in the past. The day was high-lighted by dinner on the church grounds, spread on tables under the wide-spreading live oaks.

On the walls of our home are plaques and certificates which have been given me for service. These remind me of my active days among my fellows, and bring to mind the many men and women with whom I worked. It brings sweetness to my soul. As I observe these awards of honor I will write down the wording on them:

To J. Earl Mead: In loving appreciation for one whose unusual service, gracious spirit, tender heart, compassionate soul, superb leadership and sensibility to the spiritual needs of humanity have been an inspiration for more than twenty-eight years to Sunday schools of Dallas, Texas, and the South, Dallas Baptist Sunday School workers, Fourteenth Annual Training Banquet, January 22, 1954.

There is a plaque which reads: In appreciation of J. Earl Mead, President Southwestern Baptist Religious Association – 1936.

Another: In appreciation to J. Earl Mead, the consecrated leader, dedicated Dean of Religious Education, Dallas Baptist Association, R. E. M. C., April 15, 1962. This was presented by my fellow workers at a retirement dinner given by them. It was presented by Bob Feather, President.

One plaque carries these words: Certificate of appreciation. In recognition of the faithful service of J. Earl Mead, who having served as a member of Trustees the full time allowed by the constitution of the

Southern Baptist Convention and not being eligible for re-election, is now retired from the Board. For his serious attention to all matters affecting the Board's welfare and ministry, for his cooperative spirit in dealing with the varied problems of the Board's expanding program of work, for his diligent devotion to committee assignments, and other responsibilities, for his friendly participation in an inspiring fellowship at the Board meetings, we accord our grateful appreciation. By action of the Trustees in regular session, The Sunday School Board of the Southern Baptist Convention, January 30, 1963.

There is also a gavel on which is written: J. Earl Mead, President 1959-61 – Sunday School Board of the Southern Baptist Convention.

There is a framed program: Testimonial Dinner, March 28, 1962, honoring J. Earl Mead. On it is a pen portrait of me drawn by Frances Shanks. It carries the program in which I note the following: "Insights into a Life. Appreciation of a Life. Influence of a Life by Dr. W. L. Howse. Thanksgiving for this Life by Dr. Marshall Craig." Below the program are these words: "We of the Dallas Baptist Association meet today to pay a tribute to a man whose shadow looms large in the field of Religious Education. To J. Earl Mead in gratitude we dedicate this program. Bob Feather, President, Religious Education and Music Conference, Dallas Baptist Association."

The Elder Statesman plaque has these words: Texas Baptist Elder Statesman award, in recognition of J. Earl Mead for 58 years of distinguished service to his Lord and Texas Baptists as a Minister of Education and elected denominational leader. Presented at the 53rd Annual Independence Association Homecoming, Independence, Texas, June 5, 1977.

There is also a framed citation signed by 125 members of the Boethian Class of my own church. It carries these words: Dear Dr. Mead: When an army faces the loss of a great general, one who has led it to a victory in many fierce battles, one who has had the confidence of those whom he leads, it is a sad day. With such emotions the Boethian Class approaches the time of your retirement; whether our years have been few or many, we all have one thing in common – a deep gratitude for your leadership and example. We shall all be better Christian witnesses because you have enriched our lives. Well done good and faithful servant. You have been faithful through many years of service. May God grant you many satisfying years of retirement. With all our love, Boethian Class, Cliff Temple Baptist Church.

All these plaques and certificates mark mile posts along the way as I review my life's work. In 1976 I returned to Falls Creek. There God called me into His service in the summer of 1919. I stood in the midst of the memorial garden and observed the names written there: Sue Howell, Maud Abner, Rosa Lee Appleby, Hot Dog Lee, W. D. Moore, Fred McCauley, Blount Davidson, Andrew Potter, and others. All save one had gone to meet the Maker. There I bowed my head and gave thanks to God for these men and women, and thanked Him for the years of service He had granted me among Baptists.

I have served other groups since my retirement, like Southwide Camp Managers, Texas Camp Managers, and Glorieta, which I shall say something about when I write about my years of retirement.

Blessings from
The Past Generation

I must pay a tribute of love and respect to those preceding me, as I came on the scene of action. For the most part, these were preachers. This group has influenced and blessed me more than any other. My work being in the churches brought me in close contact with ministers of the Gospel. I remember few of their sermons, but by their daily living and some words along the way, they greatly helped shape my life and gave me some things which I have incorporated into my daily living. I thank God for preachers, especially to those who made contributions to my life. Also, I owe a debt of gratitude to other older people, among them being members of my very own people. I have always revered and respected the greyheads around me.

John M. Via was once my parents' pastor in Kansas. I adored him. He was one of the happiest men I ever knew. He included me in his family reunions. I have led music for him in revivals. He was in my home when I was a young married man. I played tennis with him long before I went into church work. Though I beat him, I can still hear his laughter in defeat. His happy heart helped me become a very happy man.

Harry E. Hogan, an Associational Missionary in the Cherokee Strip, and later in Southeast Texas, was an older man whom I revered. It was he who was largely responsible for my being chosen to lead the music at Falls Creek Baptist Assembly in 1918. He was rough as a cockle bur on the outside, but as tender as a mother on the inside. When worn down by the demands of his missionary work, he would show up at our house in

Dallas. Those were precious occasions for us. Alice would give him choice food and tender care. In speaking of problems in his work which tested his temper and patience, he said, "Earl, I just had to put my spiritual foot on my physical neck." This led me in days to come to be adept in that practice.

There was John L. Bandy, who baptized me and set me to my first Christian work. He had been a railroader. He told me this story: "One Saturday I went down to the depot to get my paycheck. While there I heard a little engine puffing and groaning under its heavy load. I saw the smoke billowing up over the hill long before I saw the engine. The wheels would slip on the rails and catch again. Soon the smokestack came into view, then the front of the engine, and later the cowcatcher came in sight. I began to count the cars it was pulling. I knew the capacity for such an engine, and when I counted all the cars it could pull, there was another, and another. I wondered at the miracle. Then the mystery was solved when I saw a great eight-wheeled mogul engine pushing that little train right over the hill." How many times in later years did the memory of that story help me with my heavy loads.

I am indebted to J. B. Gambrell, the elderly Baptist sage, who wrought so well and for so long in Baptist work in Texas. He is quoted more today by Baptist preachers than any other Texas leader. In 1918, my first time at Falls Creek, I sat in Dr. Gambrell's class on "Preacher Problems." I had heard of his fame and stature and decided to hear him, though I had no idea, at the time that I would sell my business within the year and go to work for the churches. I have been forever grateful for that experience, for it was the only time I ever heard him. He gave me something that has stood me in good stead all my life.

One morning Dr. Gambrell began by asking, "Why do pastors move so often?" I perked up, for the pastors in my village church had tenure of only one or two years. I have often jokingly said, "These pastors come and we embrace them in love, then they begin telling us how we ought to live until we found it easier to change pastors than our way of living." I listened intently to Dr. Gambrell's own answer to his question. "It is like this," he said, as he stroked his closely clipped beard. "A pastor moves into a community and takes everybody into his love and confidence. When he finds some do not live right, some do not support the church, and some do not follow his leadership, he cuts them out, and moves his circle in, and in, and in, until he has to move out." This is one sermon I have practiced all my life. Some may cut me out of their circle, but I dare them ever to get out of mine.

I served with Dr. M. E. Dodd only one year. I went to him with a problem of organization. I had spent much time in study and conference about it, and reached a conclusion as to its solution, but needed the wise judgment and assurance of my pastor. I stated the problem, informed him of what was involved, and awaited his wise advice. He asked, "Have you reached a decision of what should be done?" "Yes," I replied. "Then do it," he said. I was taken aback. I expected him to weigh the matter, discuss it, and tell me what should be done. He saw my dilemma, then explained, "You are a man of God, and sought His guidance, so He brought you to His decision." What confidence that has given me in decision making!

The first time I ever heard John L. Hill was at a Sunday School Convention in Wichita Falls, Texas. His initial talk I can never forget. It was about the Good Samaritan. His text was, "As he journeyed." (Luke 10:33). He made me thoroughly aware for the first time in my life, what is in a chance meeting, a wayside opportunity, a random happening along the road of life. He caused me to put value upon what is seemingly accidental and incidental along my pathway.

I heard the senior Gypsy Smith in Dallas on his last evangelistic rounds over all continents. I was chairman of his Young People's Committee in a Dallas Revival. He was beyond eighty years of age. His resonant voice, his humility, his gentle spirit remains with me to this day. He preached me a mighty sermon in just one sentence one night. He opened his Bible and began to read: (Matt: 4:21), "And going on from thence, he saw two other brethren, James the son of Zebedee, and John his brother, in a ship with Zebedee their father, mending their nets," and here the old gypsy stopped, lifted his eyes and looked intently at the congregation, and said, "Mind you, they were mending their own nets." What a sermon it was for me! From this one sentence, I got a message for life. Since that time I have been so occupied with mending my own life that I have spent little or no time trying to mend the nets of others.

I have always been grateful that I served in the same city where Dr. George W. Truett was pastor of the First Baptist Church, Dallas, for forty-seven years. To be in this great man's presence, or hear him preach, were experiences I treasure. His mellow voice, his towering frame, his massive face, his compassionate heart one never forgets. He said something to my pastor, Wallace Bassett, which describes Dr. Truett more than anything I know. "Wallace," he said, "be kind to your people; they are all having a hard time." To me, that revealed the secret of his greatness. He always carried the hurts of the world on his heart.

But it has not been only older preachers who have blessed me. Older laymen and aged forebears, as well, have left an indelible contribution to my life.

Arthur Flake was my idol as well as my mentor. In my judgment, he made a greater contribution to the work and growth of our Sunday Schools than any other person. I have often said, "Dr. Flake was the best and ugliest teacher I ever had." There are two events I will relate, which have been meaningful to me, and taught me truths which I have embraced.

I was in Dr. Flake's class at the First Baptist Church, Owensboro, Kentucky, when he taught in the first Sunday School clinic ever held (1924). He paused to ask a question, "Are teachers born, or are they made?" Before his pupils had a chance to reply, he continued, "I was in a barbershop for a shave recently, and when the barber had finished, there were nicks on my face where he had cut me. I asked, as I looked in a mirror, "Where did you go to school?" The barber replied, "Oh, I didn't have to go to school. I am a natural born barber."

When in Memphis, Tennessee, on a denominational mission, I learned my dear old friend, now over eighty, was living with his daughter in the city. I called to see if I could visit him. It was agreeable, so a friend and I were met at the door by the daughter. We started down the hall, and I heard the voice I loved so well, coming from the bedroom where Dr. Flake was resting, "Earl, what does it take to run a Sunday School?" Then he answered his own question, "W-O-R-K, work!"

Often, when teaching, Dr. Flake would stand by the chalkboard with a piece of chalk in his hand, and when the lesson was over, there would be only one word on the board; namely, WORK.

Hot Dog (E. E.) Lee enriched my life. He was employed by the Sunday School Board. He worked in the B. Y. P. U. Department when I came to Dallas, which was the city where the Lees lived. He and I were both left-handed tennis players. We emerged as champions at Falls Creek, and later we were first in the tennis competition at Palacios. What the good Dr. Lee did in his service no one can fully measure, and I treasure the deposits he made in my own life.

I must not leave my father out in speaking of older people who influenced me. He taught me the value of toil and labor. In my boyhood, father was a farmer. One fall we were harvesting our potatoes. A neighbor came down the road in a wagon drawn by horses. We heard the steel rims of the wagon hitting the flint rocks long before we saw him. As he drew near, he pulled on the reins, and called, "Whoa!" to his team and stopped. He called out to Father, "Callaway, how's yore taters turnin' out?" Father arose from his knees, brushed the dirt from his trousers and hands, and shouted back, "They're not turning out at all. We're having to dig them out."

I will end this parade of older people and their contributions to my life by introducing my grandfather, John Caswell Smith, my mother's father. I got much of my early religious impressions from this godly saint. When I was a lad in the Ozarks, we never had the blessing at meals in our home. But always, when I would go to Grandfather's home, we would pause at table; Grandfather would bow his venerable head and say grace. He always began, "Our Divine Parent, we thank Thee for this food," then would continue to the final "Amen." For the first time in my life I was made aware of God. Grandfather prayed as if he knew God personally. I opened my eyes big with wonder, after the prayer, to try to see the One he seemed to know so well. The things Grandfather taught me about prayer and things of God have been most meaningful in my life. Ah, youngsters can learn so much from oldsters!

Later Years at Cliff Temple

Time was passing by, and my days at Cliff Temple lengthened. I was a young man of thirty-four when I arrived in Dallas, and I stayed with the one church until I was seventy. The goals set for the church were always challenging and I was content with my lot. I had a happy home, an inspiring pastor, and an appreciative church.

There is much compensation in staying at one church for a long time. One of these was my relationship with the people. Sharing their joys and sorrows, victories and defeats, drew us together with strong bonds of love and understanding. It seemed they were members of my very own family.

Our church moved from enlargement to evangelism, training, stewardship, and missions. Every year we faced these same goals, but we always tried to approach them through a new gate to attract fresh response from the workers. The organization for such programs was my responsibility.

My pastor was a builder. There was only one building when he came and seven when he left. If Dr. Bassett began to talk about building, I immediately got my tape measure and began to draw plans, for the pastor's dream was always realized. Dr. Bassett had a building which bore his name. He said, "The only building which I did not erect, and is almost falling down, is named for me." There is also a building which bears my name. It was the children's building, which was constructed at the close of the Second World War.

The church eventually bought the whole block of land, except the Masonic Lodge Building which stands on the corner. Also, a dozen lots across Sunset and Tenth streets, plus lots on Ninth Street, were purchased for parking purposes. A Cliff Temple Lodge is built on the five hundred acres which Dallas Baptist Association owns in southern Dallas County.

I was ordained to the Gospel ministry by my church on June 9, 1955. I had refrained from asking for ordination all through the years for two reasons; namely, first, I never wanted to interfere with the pastor's place, nor encroach upon his work. Second, I never wanted any handle to my name which might come between me and the people. I always wanted to be on their level with nothing to separate us. One stipulation, in my coming to Cliff Temple, was that I never be asked to fill the pulpit. They always honored my request. I was glad I did not get my Doctor of Laws Degree from Baylor until I retired, for that same reason.

My most difficult days were those following Alice's sudden death. There was no home to which I could go at the end of the day. There was no one with whom to talk over my work and its demands. Home had been my forte, my strong base, my inspiration, my joy. Now I had an Achilles heel. I felt lost. I had to work alone. Then came a day when I fell in love with Lois Harper. She was a preacher's daughter. She and her husband had been active workers in our church for a long time. Her husband, A. C. Harper, was suddenly killed in an automobile accident as he traveled for his company. Lois began teaching music in the public schools as a widow. Later she joined the Cliff Temple staff, devoting her time to visitation, and leading the church in its visitation program.

We were married, October 19, 1949, by her father, Charles H. Riddle, in her parents' home near Weslaco, Texas. For twenty-eight years, Lois has not only made a happy home for us, but also she has taken a worthy part in all my church work. Since my retirement, she goes with me to all my engagements. Building a new home against a background of no home was a dear and precious experience. With every breath I draw, I am grateful to God for home, and for Lois who makes it a heavenly place.

On my thirtieth anniversary, the church observed the event with a dinner and program. The program was titled, "This is Your Life" or "From Chickens to Churches." My father, two sisters, and other relatives were present. Representatives from other churches I had served came. Young men who had gone out from Cliff Temple as preachers, missionaries, and church staff workers were there. How Lois hid all these away and even served a meal to them at the church, without my knowing it, I will never know. Following the program, the church led me to the church quadrangle and presented me with the keys to a new Oldsmobile which they had driven to the church for this purpose. Hundreds of letters, from friends far and wide, were bound together and handed to me. These I cherish until this day.

The church desired my life's story and gathered some money for this cause. John Shanks was chosen to write it. He was our business manager and a very close and revered friend of mine. I felt the story was not worth the cost and time, but since most of my service was at Cliff Temple, they wanted the story written and put in the *Cliff Temple Baptist*, our weekly church paper.

Lois, John and I travelled together in Louisiana, Missouri, Oklahoma and Texas, gathering this information. That story can be found, as I said, in our weekly church paper.

The Foreign Mission Board sent me to the annual meeting of our Baptist Missionaries in Mexico. Mrs. Mead accompanied me. This meeting was held in Guadalajara a few years before I retired. I spoke at the sessions of this gathering and came in close contact with this able and consecrated group, which was giving itself to carrying out Christ's commission to spread the Gospel to the uttermost parts of the earth. How real the Lord was to these missionaries and how he sustained them in their work was demonstrated by the happy tears flowing down their cheeks one morning as they joined in singing, "He promised never to leave me, never to leave me alone."

In 1960 Lois and I attended the Baptist World Alliance which met in Rio de Janeiro. The church sent me, and friends sent Lois. We flew to New Orleans, then on to South America. We got a close-up view of much of Southern Baptist work in many countries, and were entertained royally by our missionaries in Caracas, Montevideo, Rio de Janeiro, Sao Paulo, Buenos Aires, Santiago, Lima, Panama, and Guatemala.

The meeting in Rio, attended by thousands of Baptists around the world, was an experience we will never forget. Lifting old hymns of the church in many languages was a warming experience. Dr. Billy Graham spoke to over 200,000 people in the huge soccer arena. The greatest demonstration of the power of the Holy Spirit in any meeting I ever attended was when thousands of listeners stood to acknowledge their acceptance of Christ as their personal Savior, when Billy Graham gave an invitation at the close of his sermon.

It must have been most encouraging to all our missionaries in South and Central America to have thousands of us from the homeland to drop in on them for a visit, and it made those of us who were in those groups more vitally interested in our mission fields. We worshipped with several congregations in these rounds. Though it was in the dead of winter, and there was little heat, we sat in the congregation with our heavy coats on, and you could see our breath as we sang. It was a genuine and blessed fellowship.

We visited many churches and joined them in prayer meeting and in worship on Sundays and felt very close to God as we sat by our new friends, unable to converse with them because of the barrier of language. We greeted and shook hands with many people, and nodded our pleasure and smiled, but after that we could not communicate.

My Guadalajara experience and the South American tour enlarged my world and brought me in touch with many missionaries. Then, too, every year from 1963 to 1970 we had been present when the Foreign Mission Board commissioned many young men and women for work on foreign fields. This brought us close to our Baptist work around the world.

Nearing my seventieth birthday I thought of retiring. I conferred with Lois and Babe concerning my feeling. They encouraged me. Finally, God led me to the feeling that this was the thing I should do. So without letting anybody else know, I wrote a letter to the pastor informing him of my decision and on the following Sunday my letter of resignation was presented to the church to become effective April 30, 1962.

The church in conference on April 25 passed the following recommendation: "It is the recommendation of the finance committee, with the approval of the deacon body, that Cliff Temple Baptist Church, in order to express to Mr. J. Earl Mead, a token of love and affection, that he be made a gift of $3,500. It was further recommended that Mr. Mead receive a gift of $150 per month, starting June 1, 1962, and be continued as long as he lives." The first sum was, roughly speaking, $100 for each year I had served this church. The monthly gratuity has been the difference between very frugal and comfortable living during my retirement. At my retirement I was presented with hundreds of letters of church members who had written expressing their love for me. These letters were bound and are in my possession still.

The only time I ever said anything about my salary was during the Great Depression of the early 1930s. At that time the church was hard pressed to meet its obligations. The pastor and I went before the church and asked that our salaries be reduced. The request was granted. The depression worsened, and we went a second time and asked that our salaries be reduced. The request was granted a second time. I have said, "Ever since then, I have been afraid to say anything to the church about my salary."

The feeling of resignation was so good. All of my adult life I had carried the load of responsibility on my shoulders. I was now free. To walk out from under that responsibility was a sweet experience indeed.

There was deep appreciation to God for my long happy years at Cliff Temple. They had been busy, pleasant years. So, as I stepped from my place as Minister of Education after more than thirty-six years, a sweet satisfaction was in my heart.

I have often said that workers for a church never retire with much money. A pastor, in his first sermon at his church said, "Brethren, I want you to pray that I will be poor and humble." Later, a deacon said, "Pastor you just busy yourself at keeping humble, we will keep you poor." I had often read that rich people in retirement gave themselves to clipping coupons. This, I thought, I would never do. But I am rich in friendships which I cherish, and I clip coupons every day through letters and words from people whose lives I have touched, saying I was a help to them along the way.

It was a daily joy to work with Dr. Bassett. There was always a perfect understanding between us. I do not remember a time when our relationship was strained. After my retirement, I wrote to congratulate him on his forty-fifth anniversary as pastor, March 13, 1963. I received a letter in reply in which was this sentence: "Whatever success I have had here at Cliff Temple is, to a large extent, due to the assistance of a wonderful Minister of Education I had for thirty-six years." He was always ready to compliment and encourage me.

Family and Personal Things

Family ties were always precious to me. Alice and I had only been married four years when I sold my half of Wakita Produce Company to Father, which made him the sole owner. In the fall of 1919 I took up my work at First Baptist Church, Beaumont, Texas, as Director of Music and Education. Later, along the way, I had to choose between music and education and chose the latter, although it was through music that I was led to dedicate my life to church work.

Home was always an inspiration, my strong base and joy. We had only one child, a daughter, Lois Maxine, who was the apple of her father's eye. Since she was the only child, I was one of her playmates as she grew up, joining her in jacks, tennis and other games. After high school, she went to Texas Woman's College in Denton. Following college she married Malcolm O. Johnson. To that union were born Mead, Martha, and Margaret, who grew up in Dallas and were members of my church. Martha married Warren Thrasher, and they are the parents of my only great-grandson, Barton Elliott Thrasher, who was born May 5, 1973. Margaret married Don Drake of Oklahoma City. They now reside in Arlington, Texas.

After Alice's sudden death in July 1948 I was alone, but sought to carry on my work at Cliff Temple. A new home was established with Lois Riddle Harper in October 1949. Her daughter, Betty Lois, was a freshman at Baylor University when I married her mother. Thus, I have three charming Loises in my life; namely, my wife Lois, my daughter Lois, and my wife's daughter, Betty Lois. Betty Lois graduated from Baylor in 1953 and married Milton Brooks McGee, also a Baylor graduate, in 1954.

This home was blessed by the birth of four boys – Brooks, Jon, Preston and Joel. This quartet of lads added much to our joy as grandsons always do. This family has resided in Conroe, Texas, for several years.

But my whole family includes more than this closely knitted group. I returned to Cherokee, Oklahoma, in the course of the years, to officiate at funerals of relatives, including grandparents, great uncle, great aunt, uncles, aunts, and cousins. Once or twice a year for sixty years, I have dropped by to visit my relatives in those parts.

Our home also became a refuge for our parents. Lois' mother, who suffered from Parkinson's disease, came in January 1953, and spent her last days in our home. Here Lois nursed and attended her until her death, June 6, 1953. Lois' preacher father, Charles W. Riddle, stayed on. We enlarged the servant's house (though we never had a servant) by taking the space from a two-car garage and creating what we called "The Prophet's Chamber" for his abode. He lived there until, at eighty, he married Mrs. Lillie Brandon in 1954, and made their home in Edgewood. They had fourteen years together before Dad Riddle died when in his ninety-sixth year.

Upon the death of my step-mother, my father spent his winters with us. There were three of us children. Father spent four months each year with each of us. How much those years of close fellowship with Father meant to me, I can never fully express. As I painted the house or worked in the yard, Father would regale me with tales of his past. He died in Caldwell, Kansas, in the summer of 1966 at the ripe old age of ninety-nine plus. I flew in from Glorieta to preach his funeral in the Baptist Church of Wakita, Oklahoma, where he was a member. We laid his body to rest in the local cemetery there, by the side of Mother who was buried in the summer of 1918. These three older relatives greatly blessed our lives by their presence in our home, and left sweet memories which we shall always cherish.

I have always taken a keen interest in athletics and games. This was brought about by my close association with young people, to whom I have devoted my life. My partner, Carroll Morrow, and I won second place in a tennis tournament put on by the Young Men's Christian Association in Beaumont in the early 1920s. After coming to Dallas, I won first place in the hand ball competition sponsored by the Oak Cliff Y. M. C. A., beating two of my church young men in the semi-finals and finals. Volley Ball also came in for attention, as I played on our Cliff Temple teams. I got my physical exercise in game competition and regular daily work-outs at the

Y. M. C. A. from the time I went into church work, until my retirement, which covers a span of forty-three years.

I regularly keep my own yard with its mowing, trimming and spading, and planting. I was aware that physical tiredness was the proper cure for mental fatigue.

A sense of humor is one of my characteristics. It has brought about laughter and enjoyment. In fact, it has occupied such a big place in my daily living that I find it often expresses itself when I am up speaking. I listened to a tape of one of my devotionals at Glorieta, and there was so much laughter, that it brought a sense of embarrassment. It would not be the real me if I deleted humor from my talks, so I try to dedicate even this part of me to the Lord.

Most of my vacations, usually taken in June at the close of Vacation Bible School, have been spent in the Rocky Mountains. I always preferred the solitude of the heights to the seashore for rest. My work has been among the multitudes, so the restless sea gave me no release from the movement and stir of the people. Daily walks in the great outdoors gave me a sense of the presence of God, as I viewed the changing scenes of his wonderful creation. Some days it was up, up, up into the high mountains in the morning and down, down, down by waterfalls and singing streams in the afternoons. Often on such tramps, Bill Watt was my constant companion. He and his wife, Pauline, often went on vacations with us.

Sometimes I would walk alone in the deep recesses of the heights to think on God's abundant blessings, to think of my coming work at the church I served, and to get the feel of the presence of God. Is there anything in the world more restful than the wind soughing through the tops of the pines, or more peaceful than the sound of the leaves in the aspen glades in the gentle breeze?

Love of nature had become a part of my life as a lad in the Ozarks. I knew where the birds' nests were, but never revealed the nests to my cousins for fear they would disturb them. I played by the singing brooks, whose waters were cool and pure, as they came from the bubbling springs along the way. Grandfather Mead and I would hitch our horses to the wagon and go to the creek banks and bring in walnuts to eat during the winter. I remember going to Grandmother's on an errand and stopping to watch the ants carrying grain along their well beaten trails to their homes. I tarried so long I was afraid I might be punished for tarrying on the way.

I studied trees, birds and wild flowers as I grew to manhood, and have accumulated shelves of books on nature for further study. It has been my practice, in speaking at assemblies and encampments, to hold up a sample of a wild flower, describe and name it, then hand it to a lady, and say, "Put this in your Bible as a memento of this occasion." I have often said, privately and publicly, that I could not see how any man, who loves nature, could be an atheist.

Once, when speaking at a preachers' retreat in Paron Camp near Hot Springs, Arkansas, I was asked to take the group on a nature walk and show them God's creation in nature. I wrote a friend, "This morning at dawn I had seventy-five preachers on their knees," then added, "not praying, but studying a bird's foot violet."

Before ending this chapter on personal and family things, I wish to add a few words concerning Eva Adams, my spiritual partner.

Once word came to me, "Eva Adams wants you to come to see her." She had been an invalid since high school days. I had never known of her. When she set the time for my visit, I wondered, "What does she want?" and "What will she look like?" I found her weak and in bed. I can never forget that occasion, for Eva was to become my spiritual partner. She is always informed of my speaking engagements. I depend upon her prayers for help and strength. We have continued as partners in the Lord's work until this day, I to speak, Eva to pray. I report to her on every return from my itinerary. Because of a weak body she is imprisoned within the four walls of her home, where she lives with her mother and two brothers; but her soul breaks those prison walls as she lifts her voice in prayer in our work together.

When I first met Eva, I found her to be a Christian of great faith in God, but she had never joined the church. I asked, "Eva, why don't you join our church?" She replied, "I am too weak to do any service, hence would only be a burden to the church." I implored, "But you can pray." It was an open door to service for her, and from her soul she penned these lines:

"A SHUT–IN CAN PRAY" by Eva Adams
Shut in behind walls of infirmity and pain,
I had known the throb of an aching heart;
I had longed to take my place in life and do my part;
"But what can I do?" I pled, as on my bed I lay;
The kindly man of God looked down on me,
And quietly said, "You can pray."
Yes.....yes, of course, I could pray;

Some of us may be blind; others cannot hear,
Some may never run and play;
Some of us cannot walk nor lift a hand to work;
But we are not empty shells of clay;
We are filled with love, thoughts, and dreams;
Our spirits are forever young and gay;
Our souls shall never die,
And we are close to God when we pray;
Yes…..yes, of course, I began to pray;
And like old Jericho, my walls came tumbling down;
Because of prayer I was a shut-in but not shut out,
For God is all around.
Why, I took part in everything!
And when I saw a prayer was answered, oh, how my heart did sing.
A fund was raised, friends reconciled, and easier was made a neighbor's
task;
Just because a helpless, insignificant one, such as I,
Had gone to God and asked.
In the drama of Life everyone is used to make God's world,
And to each he gives a part to play;
To those, who in their rooms must stay, a great and honor part is
given…..
And God always answers when His shut-ins pray.

Retirement Years

Engrossed in my Christian labors at Cliff Temple, I was scarcely aware that I had grown older since my coming to Cliff Temple thirty-six years before. As I approached seventy years of age, after earnest prayer and consultation with my family, I presented my resignation to take effect on May 1, 1962. In spite of the pastor's desire that I continue, and the congregation's plea that I stay, God gave me the inner conviction that I should retire, so I remained steadfast in my decision.

It was most difficult to sever my connections with the pastor I loved, and the people I served. The work had demanded my entire strength, which I gladly gave for more than a generation. As I stepped from under the load I had carried so long, I had a deep feeling of soul satisfaction that God had placed my life in service to my fellowman. Serving where God had chosen to put me, and the evidence of His guidance and presence, brought a joy unspeakable to my heart.

The first feeling I had upon retirement was one of release. I had borne responsibility most of my life, and now to be free from this load was a wonderful feeling indeed. My resignation ended forty-three years of continuous service as Minister of Education. I had served three churches and worked with four pastors.

I retired without plans for future service. As it has turned out, I have been kept busy in the work of the Lord, doing, in part, what I had always done, except the burden of the church was not upon me.

In the summer of 1963 Lois and I joined the adult staff of Glorieta Baptist Assembly. This assembly, later called Glorieta Conference Center, is located in the Sangre de Christo Mountains seventeen miles southeast of Santa Fe, New Mexico, 7,500 feet above sea level.

In those days, Glorieta summer sessions began early in June and ended the last of August. Our first assignment was at Thunderbird, the new and large dormitory for guests. Later, Lois became supervisor of all hostesses, and I continued my work as counselor to the three hundred high school and college young people who composed the staff. We continued in this capacity through the summer of 1970, and we consider those years of service among the happiest of our lives.

Since my advent at Glorieta in 1963, fifteen years have passed, and as I go over the country speaking, I run across these young people everywhere. Most of them are now married and faithful members of their respective churches.

From my first year at Glorieta, I became the speaker in the gardens. Our services were held as the sun tipped the crest of the mountains to usher in a new day. There the staff and guests gathered on the side of the mountain back of the terraced and colorful gardens. None who came ever forgot the occasion. Mind you, it was not my talk, but the setting and time of day, and their withdrawal to meet God which ever remained with them. I have made one hundred eighty-nine talks in those fragrant, beautiful gardens, speaking on Tuesdays and Saturdays all summer long, season after season. Sometimes I would begin by saying, "This is a quiet place where one can hear God, a high place where one can see God, a trysting place where one can meet God, and a holy place where one can worship God."

Two scenes I shall never forget. One was the quiet lines of people coming up the winding garden paths to take their seats under the pinon pines and junipers; the other, was the old songs of the church which the group sang as they went back down the mountain to breakfast.

Soon after returning home from Glorieta in 1968, my old pastor's sickness worsened. He died on October 8, 1968. The funeral service was held in Cliff Temple's sanctuary on October 10. The large auditorium scarcely contained the people who attended. The setting was as it had always been; namely, a full house, one hundred in the choir, but it was so different in that the old pastor, who had graced the pulpit for forty-eight years, was in the casket below.

I used as my text, "He being dead, yet speaketh" (Hebrews 11:4). I remembered a verse which Dr. Bassett had often quoted and had used as a text for a sermon. I think this verse typified his life and ministry. "And they went forth to go to the land of Canaan, and into the land of Canaan they came." (Genesis 12:5). He had his goal in life and nothing deterred him from attaining it. I think Dr. Bassett would have been pleased with the service because it was one of worship which exalted Christ, and had in it the victorious note of a Christian life.

It was in the fall of 1970 that I began speaking for the Aspen Bible Conference at Glorieta, and that annual assignment has continued until this day (March 22, 1978). Donald Ackland that genial Londoner has been my speaking partner there every season, he to teach the Bible, and I to bring daily devotionals. Speaking also for Annuity Bible Study Week and Chatauqua weeks have sometimes lengthened my stay at Glorieta for a whole month.

I also became known as "the Old Man of the mountains," largely because of my age and length of service. I had not missed my annual pilgrimage to Glorieta for sixteen years. Also, I had become well known for my excursions over the grounds with guests, staffers and children in my wake, teaching them the names of the trees, shrubs, birds, and wild flowers. Some said I looked like the Pied Piper walking over the grounds with groups in my train. I have often been assigned to lead conferences on nature there and elsewhere.

It was by reason of my devotionals in Glorieta gardens that I became an author. I was asked by Broadman Press to prepare my garden devotions for a book. This I did, the first being *With God in the Garden*, and the second, *With God in the Heights*. I had frequently been asked by my fellow educational directors to write a book. I would always reply, "What on earth would I put on the second page?"

My work among churches and assemblies has continued in my retirement. I find myself frequently speaking to church workers in conferences and at leadership banquets; also, there are weekends with churches where I speak to older adults. This emphasis on the church's contribution to this group is a recent thing.

The thing hard to explain about my service is that I, who gave myself to organization, enlistment and programming, now find myself channeled into the field of speaking and devotional talks. I thank God for it. I find at my age, I like this far better than working with gadgets of organizations.

There are three annual engagements I prize very highly. The first is my annual address to the Religious and Music Conference of Dallas Association. This group of youngsters accords me the courtesy and privilege of speaking to them at one of their meetings every fall.

The second thing which has become dear to my heart is that I have been asked to bring devotional talks at every session of the annual meetings of the Texas Camp Managers.

The third is that I have spoken annually at the meeting of Southwide Baptist Camp Managers. I guess one of the reasons why the assembly managers have taken me in is that every summer since 1919, I have always led groups from the churches I served to these encampments. The camp managers probably think I understand and speak their language.

I spoke first to Southwide Camp Managers at Mount Lebanon in Dallas County. I have missed addressing them only twice in their thirteen annual meetings, once at Shocco Springs in Alabama, and in Northern Michigan, where I "chickened out" because of the deep snows of winter. I have suggested that this group choose as their slogan, "Join the camp managers and see the world." Their annual meetings have been held at Mount Lebanon in Texas (1966), Shocco Springs in Alabama (1967), Windermere in Missouri (1968), Cedarmore in Kentucky (1969), Puu Kahea in Hawaii (1970), Lake Yale in Florida (1971), Glorieta in New Mexico (1972), Eagle Eyrie in Virginia (1973), Camp Caswell in North Carolina (1974), Pineywoods in Texas (1975), Ridgecrest in North Carolina (1976), Michigan (1977), and Georgia Baptist Assembly near Toccoa (1978).

I was on the program of the first Keen Age Convention for older adults, which was held in the First Baptist Church, Dallas; I also spoke at each session of the 1977 meeting. In 1977, I was devotional leader for sixteen camps for older adults. Some of these I have not missed since their beginning. These camps usually begin on Monday evening and conclude Thursday noon.

Thus, as I conclude these chronicles on my life, as I approach my eighty-sixth birthday, I am a happy man content with my lot. Lois accompanies me everywhere I go. God gives me strength and opportunity, and as time passes, "I want to be found somewhere aworking for my Lord."

James Earl Mead died and met his Maker, Jesus Christ the Lord, on
October 31, 1987, at the age of 95.
John Shanks, 2010

Part III

Concluding Thoughts
And Notes

Churches He Served

First Baptist Church, Beaumont, Texas:
Minister of Music and Education from 1919 to 1925

First Baptist Church, Shreveport, Louisiana:
Minister of Education from 1925 to 1926

Cliff Temple Baptist Church, Dallas, Texas:
Minister of Education from 1926 until his retirement in 1962

Service to his Denomination

First Sunday School Superintendent of Dallas Baptist Association

President of the Texas Training Union Convention, late 1930s

President of the Texas Sunday School Convention, 1941

President of the Southwestern Baptist Education Association, 1936

President of Dallas Baptist Association Religious and Music Conference

Vice Moderator of Dallas Baptist Association

Member of the Southern Baptist Sunday School Board of Trustees, 1959-1963

President of the Southern Baptist Sunday School Board of Trustees, 1959-1961

Secretary of the Corporation of Baptist General Convention of Texas from 1946 to the present (1978)

Ambassador at Large for Cliff Temple Baptist Church from 1962 to his death

Chaplain at John Knox Village (Presbyterian) Retirement Center near Denton, Texas, from 1979 to his death

Honors Bestowed

Doctor of Laws, honorary degree, conferred by Baylor University, 1962

Elder Statesman Award, given by Baptist General Convention of Texas, 1977

Distinguished Leadership Award, by Southern Baptist Religious Association, 1981

Personal Glimpses into
The Life of J. Earl Mead,
By John C. Shanks

Some of my favorite memories of J. Earl Mead came as a result of travelling with him and Lois Mead, his second wife, into his childhood/young adulthood homes in the Missouri Ozarks and then into Oklahoma. The time of this nostalgia trip was in the 50s, and the Interstate Highway System was just beginning. The people of the Ozarks still had limited contacts with their "outside" world. Ozarkians tended to stay home and protect their rich heritage. Even their speech sounded typical of the Ozarks.

Examples of this rich heritage include the day when we visited the little one room church J. Earl had attended as a child. One of his cousins, who was also his first Sunday School teacher, was asked where that class met in that church. We have never forgotten her response. "Oh," she said, "it was about the middle row of seats east of the stove." And when we left, she said, "Now you'ens come back to see we'uns."

But all this unusual manner of speaking seemed to vanish fast as more highways brought more speech sharing. Then came television. What was not erased by then vanished when A. C. Mead, J. Earl's dad, moved his clan to the Cherokee Strip of Oklahoma. Now it would be difficult if not impossible to find a member of the Mead bunch who still speaks Ozarkian. These Ozarkian and Oklahoman relatives and friends get much of the credit for building a solid foundation in the great leader.

All through the years I served with J. Earl at Cliff Temple Baptist in Dallas, he and I visited prospects together one day a week. One day we had knocked on a door, and while we were waiting for a response, he was thinking about and admiring some of the beautiful flowers in the front yard. When the lady came to the door, she sounded quite unfriendly as she almost barked, "Yes, who is it?" I had never seen him become so flustered so fast. His response was, "It is Mr. and Mrs. Shanks from Cliff Temple." To this day, I have never known which of the two of us was supposed to be "Mrs. Shanks!"

But he was indeed a man of love, and he loved everyone he came into contact with. When his first wife, Alice, died, he was devastated and felt so alone without his beloved wife. But, eventually, he fell in love with Lois Riddle, a widow and one of our "church visitors." She had no idea that fateful day what he wanted when he called her into his office.

"What would you say if I told you I love you?" he asked her. Lois said she was so deep in thought and so shocked that the revered and godly J. Earl Mead would have fallen in love with her, that when she went outside to water the lawn that evening, she shot water all over the house and anything or anybody who passed by. But it was indeed a love and a marriage made in heaven!

Three outstanding traits of leadership I observed through the years of knowing J. Earl Mead:

1. **The ability to think on his feet.** On the front of this book is a characteristic sketch of J. Earl Mead, with his left hand pointing upward, as he prepared to make his point in a speech. "Do you know what makes that the way it is?" he asked in a speech. And he forgot what he was going to say. "I don't believe I'll tell you," he quipped. Then, later, he remembered what he was going to say. So he said, "I believe I WILL tell you." Nobody in his audience ever knew he had forgotten a part of his speech.

2. **A wealth of knowledge on his subject.** He used to joke that he would go clear across town to make a speech not worth coming across the street to hear. One experience I had with him would make anyone disagree with that statement. Somehow he had totally forgotten an appointment. So immediately he got into my car and we got there just on time. He had organized his thoughts as we drove and gave a wonderful and challenging speech.

3. **Trust, love, and respect for his staff, church members, friends, and family.** J. Earl never left for vacation without

gathering the birthdates of those on his staff. He constantly wrote birthday letters and notes of encouragement to his staff, members, and loved ones. These dear ones were so precious to him that he gave of himself to them, as part of his life's work. I am sure that no one who ever received such an encouragement from him will ever forget that love he expressed. What a love he had for his Lord and for his people!

Remembrances from J. Earl (Papa) and Alice Mead Grandchildren

MEAD JOHNSON: My grandfather, J. Earl Mead, was a kind and gentle man. We called him Papa. He enjoyed walks in nature, identifying wildflowers and birds by their songs.

When his father needed him, he moved him into his home. Likewise, when his younger sister was dying of cancer, he made sure she had a place at John Knox Village and that he was within walking distance of her.

As a child, I remember spending the night at his home. The next morning, as the sun rose, he put on his long sleeve khaki shirt, long khaki pants and cap. He then mowed his yard and his neighbor's (a spinster teacher) front yard with a quiet electric mower so as to not wake the neighborhood.

He put others before himself and God above all. We all loved him very much.

MARTHA LYNNE JOHNSON THRASHER: I was the second of the three children born to Malcolm and Lois Maxine Johnson. Ours was a close family, full of love. All of the activities of my family, both that of my parents and my grandparents, revolved around our home, family and church. I thought all families were like ours.

We were involved in Sunday School, Training Union, RA's, GA's and choir because we were taught that these were the things God wanted us to do. One of our primary teachers and examples was my grandfather, J. Earl Mead; we called him Papa.

Papa was a very good teacher. I always felt I could go to him with any questions regarding my Christian beliefs. He had a way of making one see things more clearly through Bible stories.

He was always telling stories about birds and flowers. He knew all the birds' names, songs and interesting facts about them. He also knew a lot about flowers, especially wildflowers. His influence is most likely why I also love birds and flowers. I often think about him when I am working in my garden, remembering stories from my childhood.

Papa loved to play games with my brother, sister and me when we were children. He made little jobs into games to make our work fun. I remember having a meal at Papa and Mama Lois' house when Papa had made place cards with our names and a stick-figure drawing of us indicating where he wanted us to sit. At other times, Mama Lois would have prepared a soup or casserole to eat, and we had to guess all the ingredients she had included in her recipe. The winner would receive an extra helping of dessert as a prize!

When my son was three years old, we lost my father, Bart's only grandfather. Papa, Bart's great-grandfather, who was eighty-four years old then, would come to our house often to help me in the yard while entertaining Bart with all kinds of games. It amazed me that Papa had so much energy!

I have taught four and five year olds in Sunday School at Cliff Temple for the past thirty-three years. I only hope my legacy to these children will amount to even a fraction of what I gleaned from my grandfather. I will treasure his memory always.

MARGARET ALICE JOHNSON DRAKE: I am the youngest of three children born into the family of Lois Maxine and Malcolm Johnson. My mother, Lois Maxine Mead Johnson, was the only child of Alice Lenora Groom and James Earl Mead. My grandmother Alice passed away just a few months before I was born. When Papa married Lois Riddle Harper (we called her Mama Lois), she adopted us as her very own first grandchildren; she always held a special place in our hearts and lives. I have always felt very fortunate to have been part of a family that loved God and each other with all their hearts, and being born into the J. Earl Mead family has always been a special blessing to me.

As I read Papa's autobiography, I felt that he was right here with us again, relating his story to us in his own words. I could imagine him talking as he walked along, his eyes half-closed in thought, remembering one more thing, and then smiling as he gestured and recounted his tale.

He loved nature as part of God's glorious design and enjoyed teaching us about this world that he so loved. As I watch the scene outside my kitchen window, mesmerized by the constant activity of hummingbirds, I recall how Papa loved hummingbirds, too. He could find the tiniest of hummingbird homes, built in the most obscure locations. He loved to point out wildflowers and birds as we walked, noting their colors, songs and legends told about them. When I hear a bird's song or spy a flower that I struggle to identify, I look toward heaven and apologize to Papa for not paying close enough attention to his nature lessons!

He was always a teacher. Once on a family vacation to Colorado, I remember approaching a river. Papa spelled it out and then had us recite it along with him, "U-N-C-O-M-P-A-H-G-R-E. Uncompahgre River. It means water flowing over red rocks." That's one lesson I obviously never forgot! It is all the more significant as I read through his biography, citing his examples when, as a young student, he took part in spelling bees and other scholastic events.

He was a puzzle solver of all kinds. He loved to work jigsaw puzzles with us as we sat around the card table in the family room. We would work together on Jumbles, Scram-lets and Crossword puzzles, usually in ink! With our personal puzzles, however, he was such an attentive listener that his thoughtful comments and expressions led us to find our own answers. His love for us and his unfailing faith in our abilities made us believe that we could do anything. We always wanted to do our best to earn his already unconditional love and admiration.

He was an entertainer. He loved to include stick figures and little pictures in his letters to us when we were children so that even if we could not yet read the words, we could always "read" his pictures. When we visited he would invent games and silly voices; he was a fun playmate for a little child! Papa always had a smile and laugh for us and gave us his undivided attention. He even made games out of the little jobs he created for us around the house or garden; as he praised our efforts, we just knew that we were his most valuable workers!

As adept as he was at all things, I can never recall a time when I actually saw him drive a car! After he had passed away, I remember someone praising Mama Lois for her devotion to him, especially noting her service of always being his "chauffeur." She chuckled and responded, "Well, his attention would always have been on the birds and wildflowers, not on the road. I just drove to keep us out of a ditch!"

When I was planning my wedding, I asked him if he would perform the ceremony. He declined, as he always considered himself as an adjunct to the pastor. He did, however, stand at the altar with the minister and led the prayers. Afterwards, as he reflected on the ceremony, he said, with a little tear in his eye, "As you were walking down the aisle on your father's arm, I was thinking, that's my baby granddaughter!" He had such a tender, loving heart.

When I was around two or three years old, as the story goes, Papa was carrying me around at Vacation Bible School at Cliff Temple one summer morning as he was busily handing out refreshments to the older children and interacting with them. After trying in vain to capture his attention, I finally took his face into my hands and turned it toward mine and exclaimed, "Look at me, Papa! I want a cookie!" I did not want to share him with anyone. And yet, as the years went by, I came to understand that his heart was big enough for his family and for all of those in his extended church-family. I believe that everyone else saw him as their ideal father or grandfather figure and an "unofficial member" of their own families. And even though so many others loved him and were loved and admired by him, I have always felt so lucky that I was born into his family. It is a blessing and privilege that I cherish.

Remembrances from
J. Earl (Poppie) and Lois Mead
Grandchildren

BROOKS McGEE: At the very end of *Saving Private Ryan*, Captain John H. Miller's last words to Private Ryan were, "James, earn this." Private Ryan's whole life purpose going forward in a real tangible way was based on, would Captain John Miller have been proud of him and his actions? In other words, did he live his life to the fullest, based on what was given to him that day in 1944?

In a very real way, I hear Poppie saying to me to this day, "Brooks, earn this."

I so desire for Poppie to have been proud of the life that I have led and try to live because Poppie poured so much of his life into his family, and into me. I desire to be a reflection of who he was. And Poppie was a reflection of Jesus Christ. In fact, he was the closest reflection to Christ of anyone I have ever known.

There are so many traits and memories I have of Poppie I could write a book, but I will settle for ten:

First - His sense of humor. Poppie was the funniest man that I ever knew. His humor was never at the expense of anyone else, and he always had a joke or a story to tell. From singing "Old Granny Grier," to a never ending story about an ant moving "another grain of wheat," Poppie was a man who laughed. He never took himself so seriously that he wouldn't laugh at himself. Some people to this day think my "greatest attribute" is that I have a good sense of humor. My sense of humor came from Poppie, 100 %.

Second - He got on his knees when he talked to me as a kid. Most adults talked down to kids. Poppie got on his knees at eye level. There is a difference.

Third - He didn't preach the Gospel as much as he lived the Gospel. Do I even need to elaborate?

Fourth - He was the Great Communicator. If Al Gore invented the Internet, Poppie invented texting. He called it typing letters and I remember him typing 5 or more letters every day. He kept in close touch with scores of people. I received a letter a week from him for so many years. The influence that he had on me was beyond measure.

Fifth - He was an amazing nature lover. My daughter Harper knows that my favorite thing in Michigan is to walk in the woods. Wonder how I developed that love of nature myself? From Poppie and all the walks we had. I don't know a tenth of the trees and birds he knew, and that is a shame.

Sixth - He was a great listener. I know that part of this gift he had was because he lost his voice and was forced to listen to others. He developed it to a PhD level. A good listener was rare and much valued when Poppie was alive, and even rarer today. I do not live up to his standard - few of us do.

Seventh - He loved sports. He loved the Cowboys. I loved the Cowboys.

Eighth - He was a positive person - maybe the most positive person I ever knew. And I never remember him complaining about any health issues - just put some Oil O Sol on whatever ailed you and you would be fine in a jiffy. Life is too short to be a complainer.

Ninth - He read Scripture before our evening meals - read #3 again but don't be fooled - Poppie knew Scripture. I remember to this day some of his "lessons." I still hear his voice.

Tenth - He valued people more than things. I remember sitting on the lawn chair with him, and we would watch a plane fly over. He would say, "Wonder where that plane is headed?" He would sit there for hours engaged in conversation. Poppie was not a wealthy man materially, but he truly was the wealthiest man I ever knew if measured by friends and by inner peace.

I miss Poppie. But the funny thing is so often I still have dreams about him and I still hear that voice. If I end up being a tenth of who he was and influence a twentieth of the folks he influenced, I will consider it mission accomplished.

JON McGEE: I remember Poppie from a very young age because of the excitement I felt at getting to see him and Nanna. Some of my favorite memories were getting in the back of our station wagon and lying down in the back on our way to Dallas to go see them.

In Dallas I remember how Poppie kept such beautiful flowers. I loved helping Poppie rake up the leaves from his yard.

I think my lasting impression is that every single day you would hear Poppie typing out letters to people on his old manual typewriter. It was a daily event, and I can still hear him typing away, keeping in touch with all his many friends.

One morning at their house in Dallas, Poppie got up and walked outside to get the newspaper. As he stretched he said, "Good morning, World!" I think it was the mailman who happened to be walking by and said, "Well, good morning, Dr. Mead!"

When he would come to Conroe, I remember the walks in the woods. Along the trails, he would tell us the names of flowers and birds. I remember how delighted he was to see a Pileated woodpecker. There were still lots of them to see in the piney woods of Conroe back in the 1960s.

When we were tots, Poppie had the unfortunate task of driving Brooks and me as his passengers in the car. I don't remember if Preston and Joel were around yet. On the way home, one of us threw his jacket in front of Poppie's face and straight out the open window. That might have put an end to his driving days!

I've always thought that Nanna was the most fortunate person to have married one of the great people on the planet. She got to hear probably hundreds or thousands of his sermons and also got to hear the private thoughts of a truly godly man. Every time he came to Conroe and we went to First Baptist on Sunday, the preacher would always call on him for the final prayer to end the service. I was always so proud to be his grandson. I remember when he told me that I was his grandson but not by blood, which I hadn't known until then. I was very sad to find that out. But as far as I'm concerned, he was and always will be my grandfather. I feel honored to be his namesake, having been given the middle name of Mead.

I got to spend two weeks with them in Glorieta one summer and heard Poppie speak up in the gardens each morning. It was hard to get up so early but well worth it to hear him speak about God's creations. He so loved the flowers, trees, birds, and all of God's creations and used them in his sermons which made them so fascinating and easy to relate to. His sermons were like none I had ever heard before or since. They were so unique due to his great love of the beauty God had given to man.

I loved our walks together, which reminds me of the only time in my entire life I ever saw him angry. We were walking up one of the two very tall hills in Glorieta, and some kids on the mountain opposite the one we were on started an avalanche of rocks, and that truly upset him. Other than that one incident, I think he was ALWAYS happy and at peace with our God.

I had moved to Houston shortly before he passed. Nanna and Babe were there when I came to see him in Denton just a few weeks before he passed. I said, "I love you, Poppie." And even though he had trouble talking that close to the end, he said, "I love you, boy." Those were the last words I ever heard him say, those of love.

I always wondered how such a great man did not get more honors celebrating his life, and then I realized that that's not what it was about for him. I think he was most uncomfortable getting praised and honored, which is one of the things I love about him the most. He was not looking for that on earth. He knew his rewards were coming after he passed, and I imagine it was a celebration like none seen in a long time when he entered Heaven. I will miss him as long as I live. Believing that I will see him again gives me great joy.

PRESTON McGEE: My recollections of Poppie are numerous. In many ways his example and words have helped to define who I am. Some of my earliest memories include visiting Nanna and Poppie at their home in Oak Cliff. I can remember walking to the city park nearby and floating boats made out of pecan shells. I can remember Poppie showing me how to skip a rock on the water and helping me to climb a tree in their yard. I can remember sledding in a cardboard box when it snowed and making and eating snow ice cream. I can also remember that Poppie and Nanna took care of his father in his last years when he came to live with them in Dallas. I can remember going to Love Field late one night with Nanna to pick him up at the airport when he returned from some speaking engagement. I remember that he mowed several yards in the neighborhood for those who were unable to do so, and how on Sunday mornings he would walk to church to worship God and fellowship with God's people, and how he always had us read from God's word and pray before we broke bread at supper time.

I can remember the frequent visits that Poppie and Nanna made to Conroe to see our family. It seemed like we always had some outside project that he took on when they came down. He never liked to be idle. He would rake all the leaves or help build the screened patio in the backyard. He was always teaching about flowers, trees, and birds. He seemed to know them all and relished in seeing something new. I can remember one time when he and I rode the bus from Dallas to Conroe and him commenting only that I made his ears tired, not that I chattered on endlessly. Though he was just shy of 69 years old when I was born, I can vividly remember a 70 year old man who would carry me on his shoulders. What a metaphor for such a caring man. I can also remember actually riding in a car one time when he was driving. I can remember his special interest in my seventh grade leaf collection for science class. He wrote friends far and wide and helped me create such a fine project that my teacher not only gave me an A, but also asked to keep the project for his future classes.

I can remember the times when we got to visit them in Glorieta, New Mexico, and see Poppie at work. But for him, it seemed not work at all but just sharing his relationship with Jesus with whoever ventured into the Garden in the wee hours of the morning. I can remember the one Christmas we spent there and actually cutting our own tree from the mountain and decorating it in the cabin. Poppie loved the mountains, and I have always loved being there also. It seems that I have many times felt closest to God when I have been away from the hustle and bustle of life and been present in His glorious creation.

I can certainly recall when they moved to Denton and walking with Poppie around the lake and once again being taught and told about the trees, flowers, and birds. Though Poppie was well into his 80s and 90s by then, he was still so very active. When we would eat in the cafeteria with the other residents, he would, as was always his habit, finish eating and then spend several minutes visiting with everyone in the room. He was such a people person. When I began courting Liz and eventually married, he was always so kind to her and protective. I can specifically remember one time after we married that we went to their home, and Poppie took us berry picking, with the promise of a cobbler from Nanna for our efforts. Though he was 92 years old at the time, he would not let Liz crawl under the barbed wire fence to get to the berry patch on the other side, though it was fine for him to do so. Though I never heard him utter an unkind word about anyone, he did provide me as a newlywed man the advice that sometimes a man might need to get away and "shake the henpeck off." He was amazed at the amount of money that Liz was to earn as a first year teacher after we married, though the $16,000.00 a year was barely enough to get us through the final two years of law school when we were on our own for the first time. And he recalled how he was so blessed when he realized that the bonds he had purchased so many years before together with the modest inheritance from his sister allowed them to be somewhat worry-free when it came to material concerns. He knew that God would provide for all his needs.

Poppie's life was one that I have always tried to emulate. Though we are not related by blood, he was certainly my very real grandfather. His death, followed so closely by that of my mother just a few months later, left a void in my life. But his character, words, actions, and demeanor that I can still recall have left me with something great. His legacy is something that I thank God for often.

JOEL McGEE: I can never remember a time in my life when my grandfather, J. Earl Mead, was not a central figure in my life. When I was a child, he was the perfection of grandfather to me and my three brothers. I always looked forward to sharing times with Nanna and Poppie in Dallas and later on in Denton. He knew how to make life fun for a little boy. I remember "Joel's Garden" in Dallas, "painting" the wrought iron furniture with a paint brush and water, walks to the park, and getting to spend the night in the "Prophet's Chamber." I especially remember the week when I had chicken pox and rather than go on the family ski trip, I spent the week watching Poppie teach the January Bible Study (on the book of Job) in Pasadena, Texas. I've been skiing many times since that January, but I'll never forget that time and many other times when I had a front row seat for one of Poppie's "talks."

As an adolescent, I still liked those visits. I remember asking Poppie how to tell my good friend Wade about Jesus. I remember my first discussions with him about the possibility of going into full-time Christian ministry. He encouraged me, but was honest about the difficulties of church life. Several times he visited me when I was at a youth camp. I also had the privilege of driving Poppie, Nanna, and my mom for his last visit to see his family in Missouri to celebrate his 90th birthday. We met many of his Mead cousins and got to see his childhood home.

When I was in college, I went to Denton almost every semester during final exams to study and spend time with Poppie. During the summers I was in college, I would always make time to go up to Denton for a few days to pick blackberries and walk around the lake and talk about my future. Poppie often said that I would have a chance to "clean up his mess" as a minister. Of course, nothing could be further from the truth. J. Earl Mead had left a legacy in Baptist life that I never could have equaled.

When I was a young minister, I was, of course, very sad that we lost Poppie at the age of 95. Even at that age, he seemed to almost have died too young. One of the things I remember so well about those last few years was how often I would learn of how much J. Earl Mead had influenced so many lives. We knew him as our grandfather, but to many, many people he was their beloved minister. I remember going on a church choir trip through Beaumont, Texas, and visiting the church he had served very early in his ministry. There were people in their 80s and 90s who were teenagers when he served that church and still remembered his ministry with them. I had seminary professors who told me that Poppie was the greatest influence on their lives. My own youth minister, who was a wonderful influence on my life, remembered hearing Poppie give one of his garden talks at Glorieta. I saw J. Earl Mead's legacy in the lives of countless ministers, missionaries, and others who had the privilege to know him.

Glorieta is still the place I most associate with J. Earl Mead. I have had many opportunities over the years to visit Glorieta and walk in the gardens and hike the surrounding hills. I had the great honor, along with other family members and friends, to be present when the plaque honoring his Glorieta legacy was placed on the pulpit that still sits in the Glorieta garden amphitheatre. My last visit to the "hallowed" ground was this past summer. I had the great privilege of walking through these gardens Poppie so loved with my own family. I took my sons Landon and Grayson on the trail to Mount Baldy. This is an 11 mile round trip hike which takes about six hours to complete. As we finally made our weary way back to our car, I told the boys that Poppie had last made this hike sometime after his 80th birthday. They never met Poppie, of course, but they got a chance to be with God "in the heights" that day and were amazed to think of an old man taking that hike. J. Earl Mead was the youngest old man I ever knew.

I am no longer in full-time ministry, but I do serve my church as a layman. Anytime I get to serve, whether as an usher or a youth Sunday School teacher, or in recent years as the Camp Pastor for our Children's Camp, I am still striving to follow in the footsteps of J. Earl Mead. The legacy he left for his family, his friends, and literally hundreds or thousands of others during his long ministry cannot be underestimated. I hope that in my life I can leave even a fraction of that kind of legacy.

Acknowledgments

We are sincerely grateful to our loved ones for advice and assistance, cheerfully given, on so many aspects of this project. From questions of grammar and punctuation, to dilemmas involving computer expertise and graphics, they were unfailingly enthusiastic about lending a helping hand. Each person was especially encouraging with every step forward and onward throughout this effort, always ready to do more if needed. We thank you from the bottom of our hearts for your support in seeing our work through to its completion. And we dearly love you all!

Finally, all of the Mead grandchildren are eternally thankful to John Shanks for his leadership in getting our grandfather's story gathered and ready for the public to read and digest. Dr. Shanks was absolute in his determination to fulfill his promise to our grandfather, that his story would one day be told. Despite his own declining health, he was resolute in reaching this goal. Now, with the mission complete, we say, resoundingly, "Well done, thy good and faithful servant." May God bless you, John Shanks!

Note to Readers

On November 28, 1977, J. Earl Mead and his wife, Lois, filed papers before a notary, giving ownership and all rights of ownership of Mead's life story and also the sermon notes of Dr. Wallace Bassett to John C. Shanks. In editing Mead's story, Dr. Shanks chose to work with his wife, Janice, and with J. Earl and Alice Mead's three grandchildren, Mead, Martha, and Margaret.

CPSIA information can be obtained at www.ICGtesting.com
Printed in the USA
LVOW060253041011

248974LV00003BA/1/P